The Hidden Axis of Evil:
The Clintons, Sex Abuse, and the Aborting of America

By

Fred Martinez

ISBN: 1-4107-4619-4 (e-book)
ISBN: 1-4107-4618-6 (Paperback)

This book is printed on acid free paper.

Viva romance - rev. 07/06/04

"This is one incredible, thought-provoking book."
—**Culture Shock**

The Hidden Axis of Evil: The Clintons, Sex Abuse, and the Aborting of America

Fred Martinez

NewsMax Special Commentary Guest Columnist
During the Catholic Scandal

"This book connects the dots waiting to be connected. Fred Martinez draws conclusions others have avoided."

—Jim Holman, editor of *San Diego News Notes*

Praise for
The Hidden Axis of Evil

"I went through every single page and in full honesty it is just great. *Hidden Axis* is more than super clear and straight to the point. Every single paragraph is very rich and full of insights and information.... God bless you, Fred Martinez, and I thank you, as a priest, on behalf of the Universal Church for your book."

> —Rev. Fausto Zelaya, who studied in Rome and was ordained with a pontifical indult from Pope John Paul II

"This is one incredible, thought-provoking book.... The 'axis of evil' is being fought not just halfway around the world but also from within. *Hidden Axis* puts a spotlight on the real horrors lurking among us— who they are, where they are—and encourages us, as Fred Martinez so aptly wrote, to 'stand firm, like Lincoln, and limit the spread of a great evil.'"

> —Tony DiGirolamo, executive producer of the *Culture Shock* television show as well as the CultureShock headline news website

"This book connects the dots waiting to be connected. Fred Martinez draws conclusions others have avoided."

> —Jim Holman, editor of *San Diego News Notes*

"Fred Martinez's book is important, no, necessary reading for those who wonder how and when things went wrong in the Church and society. *Hidden Axis* is informative, insightful and constructive in that it exposes the 'cancer,' analyzes it and offers some practical solutions."

—Ginny Hitchcock, West Coast representative of Population Research Institute (PRI)

"Fred Martinez is a dedicated warrior. His columns, essays and activism have had a seminal effect.... With revealing insight and prescient analysis his new book tackles abortion and other Catholic issues head on, spelling out the problems and outlining their solution. This is a must-read!"

—W. J. Rayment, founder and editor of the Conservative Monitor

"Backed by solid research, Fred Martinez presents a moral tour de force that is must reading for those of us in the trenches of today's culture wars."

—Chuck Morse, radio talk show host, WROL-Boston

"Thank you, Fred Martinez, for specifically identifying the true 'culture' of evil in *Hidden Axis*. Asking God to bless your work."

—Carol McKinley, Faithful Voice

"Remarkable. Very well researched. A must-read for those who believe, as I do, that our culture is undergoing a profound crisis."

—Cathal Gallagher, playwright and founder of Quo Vadis Theatre

"Fred Martinez delivers plenty of much-needed 'tough love' to the Church in America today. *Hidden Axis* covers much ground, including a neat turning of the tables on the lay group called Voice of the Faithful. VOTF was ostensibly formed in response to the sex-abuse scandal and 'cover-up' and is in fact actively participating in the continuing cover-up by incessantly refusing to acknowledge the link between the scandal and homosexual priests. Included in the Martinez battle plan are ingenious ways of fighting the evils of abortion on several levels...the 'Archangel Program' alone is worth the price of admission to this extraordinary work!"

—Kelly Clark, The Lady In The Pew website

"The book is very interesting and necessary, especially for parents, teachers, the press and doctors."

—Hoang Vu, former psychology and literature professor at Taberd Institution College, Saigon, Vietnam

Dedication

My mother, Ora Martinez, died on December 6, 2003, as *Hidden Axis* was about to be released. This book would never have been written if it were not for her. She had a deep faith, which she eventually passed on to me.

At a pivotal point in my childhood, when I was abandoned and treated cruelly by people I trusted, I ran to her. I had hatred in my heart, but her kindness touched something deep in my soul. At that moment I promised I would always try to help those who need me. Many times I've fallen short of that pledge, but every time I've fallen, I've gotten back up and tried to fulfill it.

I always remember her example of forgiving one's enemy.

I grew up in one of the toughest neighborhoods in East San Jose. We had some enemies who had seriously mistreated family members. One day when a policeman was beating one of them, Mom, to my surprise, went out to stop the beating.

I thank my mother for this and many other examples of kindness and forgiveness, which helped me come to the faith.

Acknowledgments

Thanks to W. J. Rayment of the Conservative Monitor, the staff of NewsMax and the *San Francisco Faith* for their support and help in many segments of this project.

Deep gratitude to R. M. Samols for editing *Hidden Axis* and helping to give it clarity.

Special thanks to Tony DiGirolamo for his encouragement.

Also, I thank Eva, my wife, and Fred David, my son, for their patience as I wrote and researched this book.

Most of all I want to thank St. Teresa of Avila for her writings, which made this book possible. Like the philosopher Edith Stein, St. Teresa showed my poor modern unbelieving mind and heart how God exists and works in reality.

As G. K. Chesterton said, if you look at all the moral and faith teachings of Christianity, they are like a key with its strange cuts and turns that, when put in the door of reality, opens one to objective truth, love and God. Teresa's writings were the key that opened this reality to me.

If I had kept the following words of Teresa in my mind and heart more often, this would have been a better book:

"Meditate deeply these words, for it is of great profit for anyone that has difficulty in recollecting himself to understand this truth: to know that it is not necessary for him to raise himself to heaven in order to converse with his divine Father.... God is so near that he hears the slightest whisper from our lips and the most secret thoughts."

"We have no need of wings to go in search of him: let us enter into the solitude and look within us, it is there that he is. Let us talk with him in great humility, but also with love, like children talking with their father."

Above all, I'm happy to thank God who is our Father, as well as Joseph and Mary for cooperating with Him in bringing and nurturing His incarnate Son upon this earth, which again made this book possible in an ultimate sort of way.

The following verse is written in thankfulness for all who encouraged me through many difficulties and helped with this book, such as Antonio Martinez, Maria Ramirez, I. M. Lee, G. Hitchcock, L. V. Davis, Pedro Munoz, Guy Sudano, Tomas Martinez, Phillip Leahy, Dorothy Martinez, Joe Rueter, Bobby Soto, Ed Gillick, Mabel Lively, Tom Martinez, Ora Martinez and many others, as well as for you who are reading these words.

Gratefulness is a delightful experience, which by lending two hands you've given me,

Appreciation is a gift from God that takes us back to the awe of childhood's first wonder,

Admiration of good, especially the great good of kindness, is an inheritance deep in the soul,

Where we wonder at a loving Father who has given us our dearest friends and memories.

Dearest Father, please continue giving us these greatest gifts of wonder and gratefulness.

Contents

Foreword

Truth is a rare commodity in today's media. It has fallen victim to spin, misrepresentation and outright lies. But I'm happy to report that there is truth—cold, hard truth—on the pages of *Hidden Axis* by my friend and colleague Fred Martinez.

Some of what he writes is not pleasant. Take, for example, the following passage:

"Likewise, liberals replace the Constitution with sex and ethnic power struggles that lead to the breaking of the rule of law. If a president can sexually abuse women and possibly even rape them, then obstruct justice and lie under oath, are we under the rule of law?"

This is one of many points not covered in today's media. Nor is there any serious discussion of the true sources of much of what is wrong with America, such as:

- "Freud...profoundly changed America from a Christian culture to a therapeutic or self-centered culture."
- "Homosexuality is one of the causes the networks will cover up and defend at any cost."
- "It is widely known by the American Catholic Church that the vast majority of sexual abusers are homosexuals. So, why are 'Church officials' and the media not explaining that the scandal is not about pedophilia, but about homosexuality?"

These are just a few of the horrors turning our culture and way of life to the dark side—horrors which we deal with on an ongoing basis in the pages of my headline news website, CultureShockTV.com.

Unfortunately, the "Soviet Republics of CBS, ABC and NBC" bring us all the news they feel is fit to broadcast. That the networks are forces against the truth cannot be denied.

After you read *Hidden Axis* you will know the other forces, besides the networks, that for the past hundred years have driven America to a culture gravely unraveling because it is running away from truth.

Fred Martinez is one of those courageous and bold "few good men" who can handle the truth.

When I was asked to write the foreword for his book, frankly I felt like Moses at the Burning Bush. He wondered why God would choose him. In Exodus he said:

"Please Lord I have never been eloquent, neither recently, or in times past, nor since Thou has spoken to Thy servant for I am slow of speech and slow of tongue. And the Lord said, Who has made man's mouth.... I will be with your mouth and teach you what you are to say."

I have written to-the-point op-eds for CultureShockTV.com, but writing a foreword for *Hidden Axis* makes me feel Moses-like tremors beneath my feet.

I take this responsibility very seriously, because this is a good work. I believe this eloquently written book reveals the evil that is turning our culture upside down.

The "axis of evil" is being fought not just halfway around the world but also from within. *Hidden Axis* puts a spotlight on the real horrors lurking among us— who they are, where they are—and encourages us, as Fred Martinez so aptly wrote, to 'stand firm, like Lincoln, and limit the spread of a great evil.'"

Mr. Martinez has written many columns on the issues troubling this great nation. His thought-provoking work seeks to bring solutions to the problems we face. The very titles of his writing, such as his op-ed "How to End Planned Parenthood's Anti-Catholic and Anti-Woman Agenda," express answers for us to think about.

You need only look around you to see that something is terribly wrong with the road we've been traveling. Well, if you have been reading this up to now, you are that man or woman who can make a difference in the world.

Hidden Axis shows you how to help end the nightmare of abortion. It also shows you who and what caused the sex abuse scandal in the American Catholic Church as well as ways to end that scandal.

Then there's Spider-Man. "Oh what a tangled web we weave, When first we practice to deceive!" Sir Walter Scott tells us.

Speaking of webs, Spider-Man would never weave a web to deceive. The original artist and co-creator of Spider-Man, Steve Ditko, according to *Hidden Axis*, was an artist who "now seems prophetic for saying ... that if we glorify the anti-hero in art, then anti-life and violence will come into our culture."

Life imitating art? Imagine that. It has.

Hidden Axis puts this comic book superhero in a light you might not have thought about. Fred's book rings with truth, wisdom and great insight.

Tony DiGirolamo
Culture Shock executive producer

Tony DiGirolamo is the executive producer of the Culture Shock *television show as well as the CultureShock headline news website. He began his television career at an independent station in Philadelphia by producing and directing news, public affairs and children's programs. After this he worked with the media team for the 1980 Reagan-Bush campaign and has worked with ABC, NBC and network affiliates nationwide.*

Introduction

In President Bush's first midterm election, pro-life Republicans made stunning gains all over the country. Bush now knows that the backbone of his reelection is the electorate that stands for traditional religious and moral wisdom.

As I write this, African-American and former United States Ambassador Alan Keyes as well as Dr. James Dobson of *Focus on the Family*, the most listened-to religious radio show in America, have made a stand with a courageous Alabama judge for the God of the Ten Commandments.

The left and, unfortunately, it appears, the majority of the Supreme Court also have made a stand for an America that will, in stages, become a new Sodom and Gomorrah. As Justice Scalia said against *Lawrence v. Texas,* the so-called Texas sodomy case: "[It] effectively decrees the end of all moral legislation."

The sides in this threatening tragedy have never been more clear.

On one side are those who stand with the Judeo-Christian God and His Ten Commandments.

On the other side are not the other world religions or even the straightforward atheists or sinners, but rather deceptive moral terrorists who are at enmity with God and His moral law. These fakes, whose advertising jingle is "tolerance," will not tolerate the Ten Commandments in any public square.

Section One of this book shows the president and his religious supporters ways to end tolerance of unborn baby killing, which was the first stage and political foundation of the left's agenda.

Section Two shows that the fight against God and His Ten Commandments, be it promoting abortion or homosexuality, is part of the liberals' two-headed agenda of pan-sexualism and a Nietzschean power grab under the pretense of "civil rights," "psychology" and "science."

Finally, in Section Three, we show the only way to avoid this tragedy and win the victory over the Clintons–Sex Abuse–Abortion Axis.

Triumph will not come by way of wimps or even by "cool" up-to-the-minute anti-heroes. Victory will come only by ordinary people such as you becoming heroes like Spider-Man.

Section One

How to End the Abortion Agenda

As you will see, the abortion agenda began when feminists in our society (and men who, many times, forced mothers to abort their children) started running away from the nightmares that their guilt created. They did this by pretending that killing unborn babies was not about right or wrong, but about the choice to do wrong if one wanted to.

At first they lied and pretended that killing the unborn baby was only killing a mass of cells, but finally they didn't bother with that lie and simply said it was a choice.

They believed that legalizing abortion would make it okay. They didn't realize that their dead unborn babies would haunt their dreams and minds.

This section shows how the nightmare agenda began and proposes some ways to end the nightmare.

Fred Martinez

Chapter 1

How Ending the Abortion Nightmare Will Make Bush the Next Lincoln

Dr. Theresa Burke's latest book on post-abortion therapy, *Forbidden Grief: The Unspoken Pain of Abortion*, is endorsed by the great enemy of the feminist agenda, Dr. Laura Schlessinger.

Burke concurs with Dr. Laura that the feminist movement has brought us deep psychological problems, especially the abortion culture, because "if you examine the women's movement you can see that many of the women who laid the groundwork were women traumatized by their own abortions. They believed that legalizing abortion would take away the trauma."

Instead, as Dr. Burke shows, they created trauma, which brought us the nightmare culture.

She applies psychology to cure this trauma, but says that the abortion trauma can be completely healed only if one asks for and receives God's mercy. If the grief of abortion is not healed, then the world becomes a Freddy Krueger–like nightmare. Burke maintains that the horror icons of the United States such as Freddy Krueger and "evil child movies" are symbols of a culture running away from its guilt.

"I think that evil child movies are all around us. The child is the victimizer, the one who torments. Other movies, like Freddy Krueger, illustrate the horror of being tracked down by an 'abortionist' figure who is out to kill her baby," Burke says. "I've watched MTV where baby dolls are thrown off cliffs, discarded, abused and unwanted—revealing the unconscious conflict shared by all who have rejected children or been abused themselves after having been used for sexual pleasure."

The editor of *Culture Wars* magazine, E. Michael Jones, in a review of *Forbidden Grief* in the March 2002 issue, agrees with its thesis that when one represses guilt one creates even greater monsters in the unconscious. He says that "depression, suicide attempts, compulsive political activism, reveals itself upon closer inspection to be neurotic compensation for the guilt from abortion, which the culture of death instructs women to repress."

"Feminists could hardly suppress their glee when Lorena Bobbitt cut off her husband's penis," Jones says. "What they did suppress was the connection between this bizarre and otherwise inexplicable act and the fact that her husband had forced her to abort their child."

'Baby Soccer'

This is only one example of what happens to a culture when millions of men and women have the memory of an aborted baby haunting their unconscious. In story after story, *Forbidden Grief* tells us of bizarre behaviors. In one account we find a dorm party in which the students, many post-abortive, play "baby soccer."

The "baby soccer" story reminds one of a Stephen King novel, with its broken heads of dolls being kicked around, their eyes gouged out, doll cheeks burned with cigarette butts and a boyfriend burning cigarette holes between the doll's legs as well as ripping off their legs, leaving only a scarred vagina hole. This account and others convinced Burke that abortion is connected to the horror games played by our culture.

"The college students I witnessed playing 'baby soccer' were actually trying to master their trauma by belittling it through a game with decapitated baby doll parts," Burke said. "This amusement and mesmerizing allure to engage in the traumatic play is a symptom of our culture's need to overcome the horror—like the baby in the blender jokes, which all surfaced coincidentally after *Roe v. Wade* passed."

The baby soccer game and other horror genres are symptoms showing that millions of Americans need to overcome the "collective guilt" associated with abortion. Burke says, "As the group's enthusiasm for this game demonstrated, the acting out of post-abortion trauma can be contagious...collective guilt and trauma have the capacity to disguise massive injustice."

According to Life Dynamics' Mark Crutcher, this massive injustice—in which millions have been killed—can be stopped by ending access to abortion-bound women. His booklet *Access* states that "the most conservative estimates [are] about 40 percent of American women of childbearing age have had at least one abortion." There is a similar percentage of males who are post-abortive as well.

5

The booklet claims that the reason for our increasingly pro-abortion elective government is these percentages of persons who are in internal conflict. After violating the moral commandment of "Thou shalt not kill," they vote pro-abortion, seeing the stance of the pro-life politicians as a personal attack on themselves.

"What I'm saying is that since the vast majority of elections are decided by slim margins, anything which influences even a small percentage of voters can be a powerful force," Crutcher said in *Access*. "The point is that the potential impact is staggering. Moreover, this force grows considerably more powerful every day as another 4,000 abortions are racked up."

His booklet says studies have found that these women do not have abortions unless there is easy and local access to them. The vast majority of these women, according to these studies, will not travel long distances or pay large amounts of money for an abortion.

Access says, "...our opponents' ability to continue fighting comes from a high abortion rate. That is what fuels their political machine. As long as they have $64,000 an hour to draw on, and the potential for at least 4,000 new pro-abortion voters every day, the legal status of abortion will not change."

Suing Doctors

The way to defeat the abortion nightmare on the political front, according to Crutcher, is to sue doctors. And Steve Mosher, head of the Population Research

Institute (PRI), says there are many legitimate reasons to sue. Says Mosher, "The failure to stop an abortion procedure on request, or even depriving women of their right to full information, can be construed as a denial of a woman's freedom of access to reproductive health."

According to *Access*, very few new doctors want to be abortionists, so malpractice suits make the abortion business even more unattractive. As fewer young doctors enter the field, access to abortions becomes costly and inaccessible.

The abortionists and the pro-abortion media seem to agree. In 1992, abortionist David Grimes said, "Distance clearly matters in women's reproductive choices...abortion rates were found to be inversely related to the distance to a provider."

In 1998, *The New York Times Magazine* said that "abortion is retreating into a half-lighted ghetto of pseudonyms, suspicion and fear.... [T]oday 59% of all abortion doctors are 65 years old...nearly two-thirds are beyond legal retirement age."

Access presents 81 such quotes from abortionist and pro-abortion publications to show, as it says, that "access doesn't just influence abortion politics; it is the determining factor in which side wins and which side loses."

Abortion Trauma and Breast Cancer

Along these lines, another way to end the abortion government is to reach out to the millions of post-abortion trauma voters with God's mercy, as Dr. Burke is doing. If even a small percentage changes sides, as Crutcher said, these slim margins in elections may begin going to pro-life politicians. And it is never too late to start reaching out to persons in post-abortion trauma.

"We had one woman come on our retreat who was 87 years old. She suffered over half a century with this secret that she had never revealed to anyone until she came to Rachel's Vineyard. She was so relieved to be with others and to finally receive God's forgiveness," Burke said. "We can offer the Lord's mercy by not seeking to judge or condemn them, but by inviting them to thoughtfully reflect on their experience—by being the one ear that will listen, or the one heart that cries with them for the loss."

That 87-year-old woman's conversion represents millions of voters who could convert to voting for pro-life Republicans because the Democrats have steadfastly "positioned" themselves as the abortion party. The problem for the Republicans is that those women swing voters must be reached with psychological and religious help such as that experienced by the 87-year-old.

The way this can be done is for the Republican leadership and President Bush to attempt to pass legislation that offers psychological assistance to women with abortion trauma. The Democrats and media would go crazy, but if this legislation were positioned as a woman's right to reproductive health, then the Republicans would have the moral high ground.

Even if the legislation didn't pass, the mere publicity would put it into the consciousness of millions of woman in abortion trauma. The pro-life movement and conservative churches could then start offering those women the help they need.

After this is done, then Bush's Justice Department must prosecute all abortionists who, as PRI president Steve Mosher said, fail "to stop an abortion procedure on request, or even [deprive] women of their right to full information." PRI's 2002 pro-life conference introduced new legal campaigns to sue abortionist doctors who fail to provide complete information about the risks of abortion to their patients.

"We're working with these attorneys to inform more and more Americans of their rights," Mosher said. "It's time America does an 'about face' on the abortion industry. Women deserve genuine health and human rights, not violations so routinely committed by the abortion industry."

According to Pennsylvania's Dr. Chris Kahlenborn, 28 out of 37 studies worldwide show that induced abortion increases the risk of breast cancer. Thirteen of 15 studies done in the United States reported an increased risk. [http://abortionbreastcancer.com/]

The increased risk of having breast cancer after an abortion is 50 percent if it's your first baby. If you're under 18, it goes to 150 percent. If you're under 18 and your baby is more than nine weeks old, your increased risk is 800 percent!

"As soon as there comes a woman who has breast cancer who has had an abortion and takes it to court, she's got a very strong case," Kahlenborn said. "The problem is a lot of young women when they do get breast cancer die from it so quickly—because it's so aggressive when you're young—they might not make it to court."

The Demise of the Republican Party?

As Kahlenborn showed, this is not just about winning elections; it's about doing the right thing. Unfortunately or fortunately, for the Republicans this is also about politics. Any increase in abortions—as Crutcher graphically shows—leads to the demise of the Republican Party.

The midterm election of 2002 showed that even unpopular Democrats such as Gray Davis can win in high-abortion areas. And the Democrats will not hesitate to play baby soccer–type mind games with women voters in order to win.

If the rest of the country continues to become like California, the abortion state, which has one of the highest concentrations of un-recovered abortion trauma sufferers in the United States, then the Republican Party will die, as the Whig Party once did.

Although pro-abortion Arnold was able to be elected in California, nationwide the party of Lincoln could lose its base if conservatives and pro-lifers perceive that they are being betrayed. The pro-life Republican base may bolt the party if it keeps bringing forward pro-abortion and pro-homosexual candidates.

In an article titled "The Real Reason Conservatives Are So Vehemently Opposed to the Candidacy of Arnold Schwarzenegger," Texas Libertarian Eric

Dondero said, "This California race is about much more than California. This is about changing the entire face of the Republican Party for years to come. It is a struggle for the heart and soul of the Republican Party."

According to Dondero, "The Christian Right/Drug Warrior...won't stand for any Republican being elected to a high profile office who has a good sex life and makes a few positive remarks about medical use of marijuana.

"A man who once bragged in a Dirty Magazine about some sexual orgies he's had in his life and all the hundreds of beautiful women he has had sex with?" [http://allsouthwest.com/arnold.html]

Which might be the reason why Arnold—who many Republicans consider a "moderate Democrat"— was so understanding of Clinton's "human" failings. Remember when Schwarzenegger was "ashamed" of the Christian Right and conservative Republicans for impeaching Clinton for such minor failings as obstructing justice, lying under oath, and sexually abusing women? The actor said, "We spent one year wasting time because there was a human failure. I was ashamed to call myself a Republican during that period."

Some disagree that Schwarzenegger is a moderate Democrat and are even comparing him to true conservative Clarence Thomas. Brent Bozell showed the hypocrisy of the liberal media best in the Thomas case when he wrote:

"Credible rape charges are not news when levied against a liberal president, no matter how grave those charges are. But totally uncorroborated charges of off-color language against a conservative Supreme Court nominee totally dominated the news for a solid week. The national media's double-standard has descended from the merely awful to the absurd."

[http://www.mediaresearch.org/press/1999/press19990308.asp]

The media showed similar hypocrisy when the *Los Angeles Times* put the allegations of sexual harassment against Schwarzenegger on the front page of the paper, while it buried Juanita Broaddrick's 1999 rape accusation against Bill Clinton and refused to publish George Will's column about Broaddrick's allegation.

Even I, who voted for Tom McClintock, was sickened by the smear campaign against the actor, especially the yellow journalism trying to associate him with Nazism.

To be fair to the media, it is justifiable to bring forward credible charges if there is an individual with a trail of sexual harassment accusations. The problem is when they have a double standard such as in the Clinton-Thomas comparison.

So, the point still needs to be made that when the liberal entertainment-media industry gave Clinton a free pass on the brutal rape accusation and attacked the Christian Right and conservatives for bringing forward these "credible rape charges," one of the members of the entertainment-media industry who gave Clinton a free pass on the rape charge was Arnold.

Moreover, Republicans must remember that the vote was not so much a vote *for* the actor as it was a vote *against* Gray Davis. It was a protest vote against the most despised and possibly most corrupt governor in California history. As one pundit on the radio said, it was a vote against the forces of evil.

So, Schwarzenegger needs to consider that he was elected California governor only because pro-lifers and conservatives were the foot soldiers that brought about the recall in the first place and because the Democrats were so corrupt.

A high percentage, if not most, of those who did the footwork to recall California Governor Gray Davis were Christian pro-life voters. These same citizens, nationwide, may have to do the footwork to recall the majority of the Supreme Court justices if Justice Scalia is correct that the *Lawrence v. Texas* case "effectively decrees the end of all moral legislation."

The pro-life victories by Republicans in the first midterm elections showed that most of the country is still pro-life. The spectacular victories by the pro-life candidates were accomplished by pro-life voters who didn't vote for the president during his near disastrous 2000 presidential campaign because they thought he was wishy-washy on moral issues. If these voters don't come out for Bush in 2004, he is in deep trouble.

So, if the Republican Party wants to stay in power, first it must not betray its nationwide pro-life base, and second it cannot allow the abortionists to have the "$64,000 an hour to draw on, and the potential for at least 4,000 new pro-abortion voters every day." As Crutcher said, this is "the determining factor in which side wins and which side loses."

Using Lincoln's Strategy

The party of Lincoln must make a choice. They can become like the Whigs, who kept compromising on the issue of slavery until they were replaced, before the Civil War, by the anti-slavery Republicans. Or they can stand firm, like Lincoln, and limit the spread of a great evil.

Lincoln never attempted to abolish slavery directly, because he knew that if he limited its spread to only the South, then, like a disease, it would die a natural death. The Democrats—the slavery party—knew this, too. That is why they started the Civil War.

(The South was correct in its claim that it had the constitutional right to secede, and it had the Founding Fathers' idea of federalism to back its states' rights claims. This is what gave the South the moral courage to fight a great war.)

The Democrats—the abortion party—know also that the abortion industry will die a natural death if limited in its ability to exploit women. But they will not start a civil war on this issue, because they are cowards and have no moral high ground.

Can anybody imagine flabby Teddy Kennedy and company having the courage to fight for anything more than six more years of luxury at the taxpayers' expense?

So Bush can go down in history as another Lincoln. (Lincoln was considered dumber by the media of his day than our present media consider President Bush to be.) All that Bush has to do is not attempt to abolish abortion, but rather limit its spread by protecting women's health and human rights as well as letting women in abortion trauma know that he and others are there offering help to free them from their nightmare of abortion.

Chapter 2

The 30-Second Commercial to End Abortion

I've been experimenting for some time with a technique to save unborn babies. It's a campaign of home visiting, which can maybe help win more of those vast majorities of elections that are decided by the slim margins that Crutcher spoke of.

As a former producer and TV show host, I think a pro-life campaign using techniques that work in our video culture could be helpful. But the most important thing to remember is that methods without Christ are a waste of time.

In our video age, people have a 30-second attention span. Television has made it impossible to keep anyone's attention without a visual effect. So, our home-visiting program has created a 30-second commercial using a model of an unborn baby as a visual prop.

The purpose of the recited 30-second presentation is to identify the unborn child with the Jesus Child.

The inspiration for the program came when I was a sidewalk counselor in San Jose, California. In front of an abortion clinic, a female Planned Parenthood employee proclaimed herself a Christian to me. So, I asked her if she would abort the unborn Jesus.

She said, "I would."

Shocked, I just walked away from her fanaticism to think. I knew that mainstream America would not be willing to kill the unborn baby Jesus.

In two model programs, one in California and the other in New Mexico, over 2,000 homes were visited, with 90 percent to 95 percent saying "yes" to the pro-life message.

In this model program, three volunteers going out a couple of hours a week visited 1,000 homes in six months.

Imagine if there were 3,000 to 30,000 volunteers across the nation. In six months we could visit 1 million to 10 million homes.

Imagine if tens of millions identified the unborn baby with Jesus. Abortion would be doomed, first in America and then worldwide.

Remember that identifying the unborn baby Jesus with all unborn babies is true because Jesus said, "Whatever you do to the least of my brethren you do to me."

Remember, if we can convert tens of millions to identify the unborn baby with Jesus, then abortion will be doomed, first in America and then worldwide.

(If you are interested in this program, which is called Archangel Instructions, please read "How to Save Unborn Babies in a Positive Way" in Appendix 1 at the end of this book.)

Chapter 3

How to End Abortion Worldwide

The Population Research Institute (PRI) has found that Planned Parenthood and the abortion industry are targeting Catholics as well as minorities, especially the poor people here and globally, according to Ginny Hitchcock, the West Coast representative of PRI.

She said that on a worldwide basis, with the encouragement of the conservative members of the U.S. Congress, Steve Mosher and PRI are carrying out wide-ranging field research among populations in the developing world.

PRI has found that the International Planned Parenthood Federation's population control is frequently used to "subdue" Catholic populations at the expense of basic aid and economic development.

"We're building on our reputation and relationship with strong pro-life members of Congress, and Catholic leaders abroad, to support human rights and to defend the Catholic faith and the rights of Catholic families throughout the world," PRI president Mosher said.

"In 1997, we began working with the bishops' conference in Peru and with the U.S. Congress to provide first-hand evidence showing a connection between U.S. funding and coercive family planning programs in Peru. We've found the international pro-abortion movement is especially active against

18

Catholics throughout Central and South America and Eastern Europe."

According to Mosher, Catholic women in the United States are also unique targets of the abortion industry. The PRI campaign tells women of their rights under federal law to petition for full information about the physical and psychological consequences of abortion before having the procedure done.

At the 2002 PRI Pro-life Conference in Santa Clara, California, organized by Hitchcock, Dr. Chris Kahlenborn presented extensive scientific evidence that breast cancer is linked to abortion. PRI's position is that girls and women should be encouraged to sue their abortionists if they were not warned ahead of time of the health dangers of abortion.

Seamless Garment 'Pro-Lifers'

For this reason Hitchcock disagrees with some "pro-lifers" who call suing abortionists an extremist tactic or who put killing of innocent human unborn babies on the same level as such issues as nuclear war or the death penalty. She said:

"The seamless garment has never made much sense. The preeminent right is the right to life: without it none of the other issues (rights) have any meaning.... We see, for example, diocesan committees who choose to put a greater emphasis on peripheral issues...while at times neglecting the most defenseless of all—the unborn."

When asked if the ideological divisions in the pro-life movement were reflected by attacks on her mentor and friend Fr. Paul Marx, a world leader of the pro-life movement who founded Human Life International, she said that it was a matter of priorities and, in some cases, direction.

"There were ideological splits, too. Fr. Marx was an all or nothing type of person and still is.... There are a number of ["pro-life"] groups that simply will not talk about contraception and others that will not mention homosexuality," Hitchcock said.

Steve Mosher Successor to Fr. Marx

She considers PRI's Steve Mosher to be the successor to Fr. Marx in his "direction of global thinking."

Mosher's international work began in China when he was an agnostic. He saw the forced abortions and tried to get the attention of liberal American leaders with no results. Finally, Fr. Marx asked him to speak at his conferences. Mosher eventually became a Catholic and president of PRI.

His plan is to fight the culture of abortion on a global basis. In the 1960s, "population controllers" such as Planned Parenthood first obtained funding from the federal government to promote sterilization, contraception and abortion around the world.

Mosher, according to Hitchcock, wants to do the reverse: cut the funding of the global "population controllers" by documenting their human rights abuses and reporting the evidence to all countries friendly to the culture of life and human rights.

An example of this plan at work is the $34 million that was prevented from going to China in 2002 because of PRI's investigation into China's forced-abortion policies using U.S. money.

President Bush and Congress looked at the information and sent to China their own fact-finding teams, which confirmed PRI's documentation.

After PRI cuts the funding of the "population controllers" internationally, Mosher intends to go after the funding of Planned Parenthood in the U.S.

Hitchcock considers this work important toward ending Planned Parenthood's agenda, but she says this is not the most important thing.

She said, "The most important thing is what [the retired pastor of Our Lady of Peace in Santa Clara, California] Fr. [John] Sweeny drilled into me. He said if you don't pray, don't do it at all."

Fred Martinez

Section Two

How to End the Agenda that Created the Catholic Scandal

Turning to God in prayer and repentance, as Hitchcock and Dr. Burkes said, is the only way to end the abortion nightmare. But what does one do when priests and the cultural elite make the Nietzschean choice?

That is, they choose to worship themselves, their wrong choices, their race, autonomous inner "beings" or uncontrollable urges that can overpower the self they are worshipping.

Some priests and the cultural elites made themselves into human monsters who could abuse children and minors without a guilty conscience because of Nietzschean psychoanalysis. This section shows the agenda of these people and some ways to end the nightmare scandal they and the media created.

It is ironic, as you will see, that these human monsters and nightmare scandals were created by a term most think is good. As Professor Allan Bloom said in *The Closing of the American Mind:*

"[E]ducation becomes the vain attempt to give children 'values.' Beyond the fact that parents do not know what they believe, and surely do not have the self-confidence to tell their children much more than that they want them to be happy and fulfilled whatever potential they may have, values are such pallid things. What are they and how are they communicated? The courses in 'values-clarifications' springing up in schools are supposed to provide models for the parents and get children to talk about abortion, sexism or the arms race, issues the significance of which they cannot possibly understand. Such education is little more than propaganda, and propaganda that does not work, because the opinions or values arrived at are will-o'-the-wisps, insubstantial, without ground in experience or passion, which are the bases of moral reasoning. Such 'values' will inevitably change as public opinion changes."

The reason for this is because, as Bloom said, the term "value" means "the radical subjectivity of all beliefs about good and evil."

Chapter 4

Why Nietzschean Psychoanalysis in the Catholic Church Must End if the Scandal Is to End

Professor Allan Bloom, the translator and editor of Plato's *Republic*, felt that Friedrich Nietzsche was a father of modern America. Bloom, who has taught at Yale and Cornell, said in his book *The Closing of the American Mind*, "Words such as 'charisma,' 'lifestyle,' 'commitment,' 'identity,' and many others, all of which can easily be traced to Nietzsche...are now practically American slang."

But the most important Nietzschean slang word is "values."

"Values" are the death of Christian morality because values simply mean opinions. If opinion is how things are decided, then might makes right.

One must remember that whenever someone talks about values in modern America—family values or religious values or place-the-blank-in-front-of values —they are saying there is no real or objective right or wrong—only opinions of the self and its will to power.

Nietzsche's philosophy is summed up by Bloom as:

"Commitment values the values and makes them valuable. Not love of truth but intellectual honesty characterizes the proper state of mind. Since there is no truth in the values, and what truth there is about life is not lovable, the hallmark of the authentic will is consulting one's oracle while facing up to what one is and what one experiences. Decisions, not deliberations, are the movers of deeds. One cannot know or plan the future. One must will it."

As a philologist, Nietzsche believed there was no original text and transferred this belief to reality, which he thought was only pure chaos. He proposed will to power in which one imposes or "posits" one's values on a meaningless world.

Previous to Freud's psychoanalysis, Nietzsche's writings spoke of the unconscious and destructive side of the self. In fact, Freud wrote that Nietzsche "had a more penetrating knowledge of himself than any other man who ever lived or was likely to live."

Max Weber and Sigmund Freud are the two writers most responsible for Nietzschean language in America. Few know that Freud was "profoundly influenced by Nietzsche," according to Bloom. Freud, much more than Weber, profoundly changed America from a Christian culture to a therapeutic or self-centered culture.

The therapeutic approaches, which started with Freud, have a basic assumption that is not Christian. The starting point is not the Christian worldview, which is summed up in the parable of the prodigal son: a fallen and sinful world with persons needing God the Father to forgive them so they can return to be His sons and daughters.

Unlike the Christian worldview, the therapeutic starting point is that the individual must overcome personal unconscious forces, in Freud, and in Jung the person must unite with the collective unconscious, which is shared by all humans.

In both cases the therapist assists his client to change himself to 'become his real self.' Forgiveness and returning to God are not needed. What is needed, instead of God and His forgiveness, is a therapist assisting a self to reach the fullness of itself.

Under the influence of Nietzsche, Freud moved psychiatry away from the mechanistic and biological to the previously "unscientific" model of the "symbolic language of the unconscious."

Carl Jung, Freud's pupil, took the symbolic language of the unconscious a step further. Unlike his mentor, Jung's unconscious theory is not just about making conscious one's sexually repressed or forgotten memories. His symbolic therapy used what he called the "active imagination" to incorporate split-off parts of the unconscious (complexes) into the conscious mind.

He believed with Freud that dreams and symbols are means to the unconscious, but for Jung the dream and symbol are not repressed lusts from stages of development. They are a way to unite with the collective unconsciousness.

Many Christians thought this "language of the soul" was a step forward from what they considered the cramped scientific reality of modernity. What they didn't understand was that Jung's theory was part of a movement that led to the rejection of objective morality and truth.

Jungian (and Freudian) psychoanalysis reduces Christian concepts such as God, free will and intelligence to blind reactions, unconscious urges and uncontrollable acts. Even more disastrous, Jung inverted Christian worship.

Leanne Payne, a Christian therapist, considers Jung, rather than a scientist, to be a post-modernist subjectivist. Jung's active-imagination therapy "is hostile not only to the Judeo-Christian worldview but also to all systems containing objective moral and spiritual values. Within this world the self becomes god. What the self wants is what is finally right or moral." (*The Healing Presence*, page 251)

Payne said that "these psychic personae [complexes] are literally called 'gods' (archetypes), and so an overt idolatry of self follows quickly." (*Listening Prayer*, page 215)

Within the modern French Nietzschean schools of thought, a type of Jungian unconscious urge is replacing the old existential conscious self who chooses. The post-modernist is moving from the idolatry of self to the idolatry of autonomous inner "beings" that, according to Payne, are similar to pagan "gods."

As C. S. Lewis predicted in *The Screwtape Letters*, we are moving to a "scientific" paganism. C. S. Lewis's name for the "scientific" pagan is the Materialist Magician, and the name of the autonomous inner "beings" is "Forces."

In *The Screwtape Letters*, his character, who is a senior evil spirit, says:

"I have high hopes that we shall learn in due time how to emotionalise and mythologise their science to such an extent that what is, in effect, belief in us (though not under that name) will creep in while the human mind remains closed to the Enemy [God]. The 'Life Force,' the worship of sex, and some aspects of Psychoanalysis may here prove useful. If once we can produce our perfect work—the Materialist Magician, the man, not using, but veritably worshipping, what he vaguely calls 'Forces' while denying the existence of 'spirits'—then the end of the war will be in sight."

Some of the largest audiences for this "scientific" paganism with its inversion of worship and the Judeo-Christian worldview are followers of Christ. By using Christian symbols and terminology, Jungian spirituality has infiltrated to a large extent Christian publishers, seminaries, even convents and monasteries.

Many Christians are using Jung's active imagination as a method of prayer. Psychiatrist Jeffrey Satinover, M.D., thinks this is dangerous because "this fantasy life has no moral underpinnings, because it helps to reinforce an experience of autonomous inner 'beings' accessible via the imagination, and because it is a defense against redemptive suffering, it easily allies with and quickly becomes a Gnostic form of spiritually with powerfully occult overtones." (*Crisis of Masculinity*, page 129, in Appendix)

If one is under the influence of the autonomous inner "beings," uncontrollable urges can overpower the self. One can go temporarily or permanently insane. And in the Christian worldview, the autonomous inner "being" is not always just an imaginary being, but can be a personal being, which then makes possession a rare, but not impossible, occurrence.

In fact, according to one Jungian therapist, Nietzsche himself went insane permanently when an autonomous inner "being" (archetype) overpowered him. So, unfortunately with the widespread acceptance of Jungian spirituality, mainstream Christianity seems to be moving to post-modern Nietzschean insanity and possibly, in some cases, possession.

Jung's autobiography is full of insane or occult experiences. He was continually hearing voices. In his autobiography he said his home was "crammed full of spirits. They were packed right up deep to the door, and the air was so thick it was scarcely possible to breathe." (*Memories, Dreams, Reflections*, pages 215–216, Fontana, London, 1993)
[http://www.quodlibet.net/brabazon-challenge.shtml]

During the Hitler regime, which itself was deeply influenced by Nietzsche as well as obsessed with the occult, Jung edited a Nazi psychotherapeutic journal in which he said, "The 'Aryan' unconscious has a higher potential than the Jewish." Keep that word "potential" in mind; it is used by American psychology. In fact, that word became a psychological movement based on Nietzsche's concept of "will to power," in which Supermen, or superior persons, "strive" to "realize" their "potential."
[http://www.geocities.com/savepenry/nazi.html]

As in the Nazi regime, once opinion is master, then might makes right. In *Beyond Good and Evil*, Nietzsche proclaimed a new morality, "Master morality," which was different from Christian morality—or "slave morality," as he called it. He thought the weak have the morality of obedience and conformity to the master. Masters have a right to do whatever they want; since there is no God, everything is permissible.

That Hitler was enraptured by the teachings of the author of *Beyond Good and Evil* is shown by William L. Shirer:

"Nazi scribblers never tired of extolling him [Nietzsche]. Hitler often visited the Nietzsche museum in Weimar and publicized his veneration for the philosopher by posing for photographs of himself staring in rapture at the bust of the great man." (*The Rise and Fall of the Third Reich*, page 146)

Both Germany and Christianity, throughout its history, have much to be sorry about in their treatment of the Jewish people. Pope John Paul II, a couple of years ago, rightly made a formal apology for those Christians in history who were anti-Semitic, contrary to the moral teachings of Jesus Christ.

However, the pagan Hitler and atheist Nietzsche need not apologize for going contrary to their teachings, because they were only taking their "values" to their logical conclusion. As Mona Charen said in the *Jewish World Review*:

"While some Jews have explicitly blamed Christians or Catholics for the atrocities of the Nazi regime, few Jewish scholars share that simplistic view. Christian Europe was anti-Jewish for 19 centuries, and this contempt and hatred often flared into violence, theft of Jewish property, expulsion and massacres. In 1215, the Fourth Lateran Council required humiliating clothing for Jews, and it was the Church itself that first confined Jews within ghettoes in Italy. The antipathy was bipartisan, embraced by Catholics and Protestants alike. After an initial flirtation with the Jews, Martin Luther condemned them brutally after he saw that they would no more follow him than bow to the Church in Rome.

"Abhorrent as it was, Christian anti-Semitism was never genocidal. As Professor Ascheim of Hebrew University in Jerusalem put it: 'The aim of the Christian was to convert the Jew. This was the worst nightmare of the Nazi.' Nazism, with its specious racial theories and pagan worship of nation and blood, was something new, transgressive and different. Nazism loathed the Jews but also disdained Christianity with its 'effeminate pity-ethics.'"
[http://www.jewishworldreview.com/cols/charen031500.asp]

It is easy to see why Hitler admired Nietzsche's denial of the Judeo-Christian God of the Ten Commandments when one considers Nietzsche's masterpiece, *Thus Spake Zarathustra*, in which he said the new masters would replace the dead God. The masters were to be called Supermen, the superior men.

After Freud and Jung came Alfred Adler, also a follower of Nietzsche, with "Individual Psychology," saying that the person strives for what he called "superiority" and what many in American psychology call potential. Nietzsche's "will to power" has been changed into the psychological idea of "self-actualization," where the person strives to realize his "potential."

According to Washington State University Professor Paul Brians' essay "The Influence of

Nietzsche," the "entire" human potential movement is indebted to Nietzsche:

"Alfred Adler (1870–1937) developed an 'individual psychology' which argues that each individual strives for what he called 'superiority,' but is more commonly referred to today as 'self-realization' or 'self-actualization,' and which was profoundly influenced by Nietzsche's notions of striving and self-creation. The entire 'human potential movement' and humanistic psychology (Abraham Maslow, Carl Rogers, Rollo May, etc.) owes a great debt to this line of thought. Even pop psychologists of 'self-esteem' preach a gospel little different from that of Zarathustra."

[http://www.wsu.edu:8080/~brians/hum_303/nietzsche.html]

Mary Kearns, in an address to the Catholic Head Teachers Association of Scotland, spoke of the Nietzschean ideas now being taught in Catholic schools in the name of "scientific" psychology. Kearns said:

"The methods are based on the 'group therapy technique' first developed in America in the 1970s by two psychologists, Carl Rogers and Abraham Maslow. They described how emotional conditioning should be carried out by a group 'facilitator.' The facilitator does not impart knowledge like the old-fashioned teacher. Instead, he/she initiates discussions encouraging children to reveal their personal views and feelings. The facilitator's approach is 'value free.' There is no right or wrong answer to any religious or moral question. Each person discloses what is right or wrong for them. All choices are equally valid even if they are opposites. Everything depends on feelings or emotions. Reason and conscience are discouraged. If anyone attempts objective evaluation, they are to be treated as an 'outsider' and there will be a strong emotional reaction against such 'judgmental intolerance.'"

If it is true that Catholic education now uses these techniques in teaching religious and moral education, then the Catholic education system has entered into the Nietzschean insanity. If these are the techniques being used in education and in the seminaries, then sexual misconduct charges against priests are a symptom of "scientific" paganism replacing Christianity.

Santa Rosa, California, priest Don Kimball, who has been convicted of sexual molestation, is an example of someone whose "approach" was "value free"—that is, there was "no right or wrong answer to any religious or moral question."

In 1996, Karyn Wolfe and Mark Spaulding of Pacific Church News said: "THE WEDGE! You can't do youth ministry (any ministry for that matter) without it.... Basing his theory on psychologist Abraham Maslow's 'Hierarchy of Needs', the Rev. Don Kimball developed this model for the growth and maturity process of a group."

Another example of someone using the "value-free" approach is Thomas Zanzig, a major leader in the Catholic Church for youth ministry, plus an editor and writer of Catholic textbooks.

According to a 1997 essay, "Models for Senior High Youth Ministry: Teaching in the Church," by Marks S. Winward, "Zanzig bases his 'Wedge Model' on a similar model developed by Fr. Don Kimble."

Homeschool leader Marianna Bartold said, "Sharing the Christian Message [a four-year religious education program for high school students] by Thomas Zanzig has students come up with as many slang or street words as possible for penis and vagina in three or four minutes."

[http://members.tripod.com/~catholic_homeschool/divided.html]

Now, many might say these are only isolated cases of misuses of Maslow and Adler—until one reads the original text. According to William Coulson, who formerly collaborated with Carl Rogers, "Maslow was always a revolutionary.... In 1965, working a radical idea about children and adult sex into his book about management, *Eupsychian Management: A Journal*, [Maslow said]: 'I remember talking with Alfred Adler about this in a kind of joking way, but then we both got quite serious about it, and Adler thought that this sexual therapy at various ages was certainly a very fine thing. As we both played with the thought, we envisioned a kind of social worker...as a psychotherapist in giving therapy literally on the couch.'" (Quote from "A Diabolical Enterprise: Maslow Was the Culprit" by Eric Reslock in the June 2000 *San Francisco Faith*)

As one can see, that basic therapeutic assumption leads to certain results in the real world.

These thinkers don't believe in the basic Christian starting point that there is a need for forgiveness from God. Instead, they believe there is no sin, only selves needing to reach the fullness of themselves.

It is understandable that atheists such as Nietzsche, Maslow and Adler could hold these basic assumptions,

Fred Martinez

but that Christians and priests also hold these assumptions is a disgrace. The denial of original sin and personal sin is, in large part, behind the headlines of the Boston catastrophe and other dioceses.

The failure of these Catholic bishops is a failure to teach the faith and moral teachings of Jesus Christ. Getting rid of a few priests will not solve the problem if these basic assumptions stay, because more—only cleverer—sex abusers will rise up to take their place.

I feel sorry for these bishops and other Church leaders if they don't take a look at themselves and repent of these basic assumptions in their dioceses. They must eventually come face to face with the Living God. He is the Father of these little ones who have been scandalized and abused.

Chapter 5

Why Certain Media Marketing and Management Tactics Must Be Fought if the Church Scandal Is to End

After 9/11, certain Muslims had to come face-to-face with the Living God for their slaughterhouse terrorism. Meanwhile, the Nietzschean media decided to play games with the American populace.

Through marketing techniques, the American media, after 9/11, presented Muslims as the victims of hate crimes. They used marketing techniques again when, after the Boston church scandal, they showed us images of sex abuse victims followed immediately by images of priests in Roman collars.

The advertising plan was to associate all Catholic priests with sex abuse, in order to destroy the Catholic faith. The networks wanted to make this into a "crisis of faith." This is why ABC anchorman Peter Jennings could say, "There are those who argue that this may be, in many respects, the beginning of the end of the clerical culture—in other words, the culture of the priests and the bureaucracy running the priests."

The Muslim "victim images" showed us the networks' marketing plan, which was to associate terrorism with only a small group outside the Islamic mainstream. This strategy is why ABC's Jennings didn't say something like "There are those who argue that this may be, in many respects, the beginning of the

Fred Martinez

end of the Islamic culture—in other words, the culture of the Muslims and the bureaucracy running Islam."

Media Bias against Catholicism

Nor did the networks, after 9/11, come close to saying what William Safire wrote in his column on October 2, 2001: "The suicide bombers were motivated to mass murder by the false promise of eternal joy after death, and it is up to Muslim clergy—who know their Koran and have special credibility—to publicly and repeatedly refute that cultish brainwashing."

Why do the pro-abortion, pro-homosexual media viciously attack the one religion while giving the other fair and even favorable coverage? It would seem that both religions would be attacked equally, since both consider abortion and homosexuality wrong.

The answer lies, in part, in the economic interests of those who control the networks. They cannot afford to alienate the Islamic people of the Middle East, who hold much of the world's oil and natural gas reserves upon which our economy depends. Catholics hold no such material strategic interest.

The Catholic Church does hold moral strategic interests that concern the media. To find out what those moral concerns are, one only need look at the one Muslim that the media vilified as much as the Catholic priesthood—John Walker Lindh. The media covered up the psychological reason Lindh rejected the liberalism of his father (and the networks). He became a Muslim when his dad divorced his mom to move in with a homosexual.

Homosexuality is one of the causes the networks will cover up and defend at any cost. They know they must discredit the Catholic Church because if even a small percentage of the Catholics in the United States returned to the true faith and objective morality of their religion and voted accordingly, then the small margins of victories by liberal politicians would be lost. The media's homosexual agenda on the political front would be lost for another generation.

That is the reason why they are repressing, for the most part, the unquestionable fact that the Catholic scandal is not about pedophilia; it's about homosexuality.

Sometimes, however, there are cracks in the media's suppression of facts.

In 2002, *U.S. News & World Report* columnist John Leo reported that studies have shown that 5 percent of priests or fewer fit the pedophile description. He said, "Most sexual victims of priests are teenage boys, according to one estimate. A study of Chicago's 2,200 priests identified 40 sexual abusers, only one of whom was a pedophile."

It is widely known by the American Catholic Church that the vast majority of sexual abusers are homosexuals. So, why are "Church officials" and the media not explaining that the scandal is not about pedophilia, but about homosexuality? Leo says, "Most likely because opening up the issue of sexually active gay priests is itself explosive, even apart from charges of abuse."

American Church Is in Civil War

The reason homosexuality is "explosive" is not just because of the media's attack slogans of homophobia and intolerance, but also because the American Catholic Church is a house divided—about to explode apart. The American Church is in civil war.

On one side you have those who follow Rome and its objective faith and moral teaching. On the other side are the liberals who reject objective morality and replace it with "value language," which originated with Friedrich Nietzsche. They use psychological and civil rights jargon, but their Nietzschean "value language" has led them to relativism and will to power.

Professor Allan Bloom, author of *The Closing of the American Mind*, said the only virtue that 50 years of Nietzsche's influence on public education—and, he could have added, 30 years of Catholic education—has achieved is relativity of truth. Bloom said relativism "is the modern replacement for the inalienable natural rights that used to be the traditional ground for a free society."

The move away from objective truth leads to universal rights being replaced by Nietzsche's will to power. Bloom, for example, showed how the old civil rights movement "relied on the Declaration of Independence and the Constitution." But the Black Power movement considered the Constitution "corrupt" and demanded a "black identity, not universal rights. Not rights but power counted."

The liberal "Catholics" speak the jargon of the Catholic while following Nietzsche's will to power. They understand power and hold most of the power positions in the infrastructure of the American Church. According to Catholic scholar James Hitchcock, the leftist "clerical homosexual network" extends to "bishops, seminary rectors, chancery officials, [and] superiors of religious orders." (June 2002 issue of *The Catholic World Report*)

The orthodox Catholics, the ones not infected with relativism and will to power, not realizing that their opponents use words as a ploy to attain power, still use logic in an attempt to reason them back to objective truth. So they control many publications, as well as the EWTN Cable Network, but they have power over only a few dioceses, colleges and high schools, where the real power is.

Meanwhile, the Nietzschean "Catholics" are going for the throat by going after the young. They control the American Catholic high school system, which is pro-homosexual, and filter out Roman Church documents such as the Catechism of the Catholic Church. The Catechism states that "homosexual acts are intrinsically disordered...[and] under no circumstances can they be approved."

That the Catholic schools are not teaching the objective morality of the Catechism of the Catholic Church is shown by recent polls which found that the vast majority of Catholic high school students are pro-gay. That is, they buy the whole gay agenda and even have gay clubs at their Catholic schools.

Fred Martinez

Leftists Reject Objective Truth

Norman Mailer, in his book *The Prisoner of Sex*, shows why orthodox Catholics must fight the Nietzschean "Catholic's" will to power and moving away from the sexual teaching of the Catechism of the Catholic Church, such as that heterosexual sex within marriage must be the norm for a healthy society:

"So, yes, [homosexuals] in prison strive to become part of the male population, and indeed—it is the irony of homosexuality—try to take on the masculine powers of the man who enters them, even as the studs, if Genet is our accurate guide, become effeminate over the years.... Homosexuality is not heterosexuality. There is no conception possible, no, no inner space, no damnable spongy pool of a womb...no hint remains of the awe that a life in these circumstances can be conceived. Heterosexual sex with contraception is become by this logic a form of sexual currency closer to the homosexual than the heterosexual, a clearinghouse for power, a market for psychic power in which the stronger will use the weaker, and the female in the act, whether possessed of a vagina or phallus, will look to ingest or steal the masculine qualities of the dominator."

This is the end result when universal truths and responsibility toward those truths are denied. The only "currency" remaining to the left is stealing power, because they are insecure in any truth, including their own objective masculinity or femininity.

Unsure of their own objective masculinity or femininity—or any objective truth, for that matter—

they will not tolerate truth, calling it intolerance. They will not tolerate the truth of the purpose of sex, which is married love, with the creation of a secure family for the children of that love.

Leftists both within and outside the Catholic Church replace the traditional family with sexual power struggles that lead to the death mills of the abortion industry, the graveyards of AIDS, and the abandonment of children and women at the altar of free sex.

Sex is not free. It was once a responsibility that a mature man entered into for life, for the security of his beloved children and wife.

Clintonian Power Tactics

Likewise, American liberals replace the Constitution with sex and ethnic power struggles that lead to defying the rule of law. If a president can sexually abuse women and possibly even rape them, then obstruct justice and lie under oath, are we under the rule of law? If our society will not tolerate truth, then men and women are not secure in their "inalienable natural rights that used to be the traditional ground for a free society," as Bloom said.

If we reject the rule of law and natural rights, our society will progress toward the Clintonian power tactics of prison homosexuals and, as we will see, political prisons. The leftists in the Church and the media who reject objective truth no longer want to be identified as persons of objective faith and reason, but rather as Nietzschean post-modernists associated with the "culture" of the gay and Clintonian playboy slogans of the media elite.

The media elite use marketing techniques on anyone who wants to be identified as a person with objective morals, faith and reason. The media redefine the meaning of words like morals, faith and reason through association and repetition, then isolate those who don't accept the new definitions, after which they ostracize any person or group that doesn't accept the new "culture" and isn't a "team player."

The very respected scholar Edgar H. Schein of the MIT Sloan School of Management explains the process in his paper "Organizational Learning as Cognitive Re-definition: Coercive Persuasion Revisited":

"It may seem absurd to the reader to draw an analogy between the coercive persuasion in political prisons and a new leader announcing that he or she is going 'to change the culture.'

"However, if the leader really means it, if the change will really affect fundamental assumptions and values, one can anticipate levels of anxiety and resistance quite comparable to those one would see in prisons. The coercive element is not as strong. More people will simply leave before they change their cognitive structures, but if they have a financial stake or a career investment in the organization, they face the same pressure to 'convert' that the prisoner did."

[http://www.sol-ne.org/res/wp/10010.html]

By using this process, the leftists, with the media's marketing ability, learned they could create massive peer pressure—some would call it a "mob mentality," which changes the worldview of people with weak morals, weak faith or the Judas mentality. These types of people see themselves as the "elite" or Nietzschean Supermen because they accept the "culture of teamwork" and have "openness" to the new definitions.

These persons wishing to be part of the "culture" or "team" are open to "cognitive re-definition." Schein explains how the process works:

"'Cognitive re-definition' involved two different processes. First, concepts like crime and espionage had to be *semantically redefined*. Crime is an abstraction that can mean different things in different conceptual systems when one makes it concrete. Second, standards of judgment had to be altered. Even within the western concept of crime, what was previously regarded as trivial was now seen to be serious. The anchors by which judgments are made are shifted and the point of neutrality is moved. Behavior that was previously judged to be neutral or of no consequence became criminal, once the anchor of what was a minimum crime was shifted. These two processes, semantic re-definition and changing one's anchors for what is good or bad, acceptable or unacceptable, are the essence of cognitive re-definition."

[http://www.sol-ne.org/res/wp/10010.html]

Tough Love Needed to Overcome 'Cognitive Re-definition'

Some orthodox Catholic priests are falling into cognitive re-definition because of their desire to be in

45

the "culture of teamwork." James Hitchcock said in the June 2002 issue of *The Catholic World Report*, "There is an obvious sense of clerical elitism in terms of the priestly state itself, which sometimes causes orthodox priests to protect their unorthodox brethren...who feel strong bonds of loyalty to one another and are reluctant to acknowledge misconduct by residents of those rarified circles."

It is time for all priests, bishops and laypersons to decide if they want to be "loyal" to the leftists' media-created "team" or to the Church of Jesus Christ. It is time for all people of good will and all faiths to refuse to participate in "coercive persuasion."

Catholics will save their American branch of the Church and Americans will save their "inalienable natural rights" and free society only by first praying for wisdom and then using that wisdom to join all people of good will to expose and engage the liberal media—not with slogans, but with objective morals, faith, reason and tough love.

Rome was conquered by the Christians in this way. Our country, as well as our children and their children, are depending on us to give them this tough love.

They need to hear us say that objective morality, such as chastity before and after marriage, is the only solution for our despairing society. They need to hear us say that sex outside the purpose of family life, be it heterosexual or homosexual, is a grave sin.

Chapter 6

How to End the Church Scandal and Priest Shortage

Steve Mosher, head of the Population Research Institute (PRI), said that the media are "misrepresenting" and "exaggerating" the "pedophilia crisis" in the Catholic Church.

According to him and other speakers at PRI's pro-life conference in Santa Clara, California, in 2002, a major problem in the American Catholic Church, and specifically in the San Francisco Bay Area, is homosexuality.

Mosher contended that the present Church crisis is not about pedophilia, but about homosexuality.

"Only a tiny fraction of the priesthood has ever been guilty of this kind of indiscretion [pedophilia]. The vast majority [of priests accused of sex abuse are] engaging in homosexual acts with young men after the age of puberty. True pedophilia is very rare," Mosher said.

"This is not pedophilia if it is past puberty. These are priests who are acting out on homosexual impulses and preying on adolescent young men. So you have to understand that is why the Vatican is saying homosexuals shouldn't be ordained into the priesthood."

The Vatican, according to Mosher, has always considered homosexuality to be a grave sin and therefore has said that men with that inclination should not to be allowed into the priesthood.

He said that the Church wants to protect young men who could become victims of homosexual predators. At the same time it also seeks to protect young men who might become predators by keeping them out of a role in which they could abuse their authority.

He thinks these and other homosexuals need to be reached out to with the message of God's mercy:

"We need to reach out to people of homosexual inclination with the same message of the gospel that I was reached with when I was a sinner. I don't claim any moral superiority here. I think all grave sins are potentially fatal to the soul. I was reached by my wife and children, but I think when you become a member of a subculture, it's very difficult to reach you. We need to reach people like that with a message that will not only save their soul, but, with the scourge of AIDs as well, save their lives."

Mosher related that this issue was of "particular concern" to him because he has a sister who, after a bad marriage, went to San Francisco and became part of the lesbian community. He said, "We are still praying for her today. So this is an issue that has touched our lives."

According to Dr. Stanley Monteith, M.D., an author and talk show host in Northern California, the "tragedy" is that a lot of people are "trapped" in this lifestyle with no hope of getting out.

"They are being told, 'You can't get out of this. You are born this way.' But the average homosexual needs to be told that God loves him. They can leave that lifestyle anytime they want because they weren't born that way," Monteith said.

"It becomes a sexual addiction, but they can get out of the gay lifestyle. If they couldn't, then how did Ellen DeGeneres' partner just happen to leave her and marry a man? No one wants to point that out, because if she was born that way, why is she married now?"

The Catechism of the Catholic Church agrees with Monteith when it states in section 2357 that "homosexual acts are intrinsically disordered...under no circumstances can they be approved." Nowhere in the Catechism is there the "political agenda" that presumes an "unchangeable" biological or genetic basis for acts it calls "intrinsically disordered."

"The argument over genetics is a curious one. If homosexuality is genetically inherited, then... [i]dentical twins must be either both heterosexual or both homosexual, and we know this is not the case. It has been documented in cases of identical twins where only one was homosexual," said Dick Frost, director of the Department of Family Life for the Diocese of Duluth, Minnesota. "Biologically, two men do not fit together to procreate, nor do two women. Biologically, it is impossible."

Moreover, Dr. Monteith said that there is a difference between being homosexual and being gay. When one is homosexual, there is a same-sex attraction, but when the term gay is used, one becomes part of a "political agenda." According to him, the Church pedophilia crisis is part of the media's political

Fred Martinez

agenda to discredit the Catholic Church because of its stance on homosexuality and other moral issues.

"This is being exploited and media-driven to actually challenge the faith of Catholics," Monteith said. "My Protestant faith wasn't broken by Jimmy Swaggart and Jessie Jackson and other ministers who have betrayed their calling."

Dr. Alice von Hildebrand, an internationally known philosopher, agreed with the doctor. She said priests who have betrayed their calling wouldn't break the faith of Catholics. But she did give a stern message to the American bishops.

"He permitted Judas to betray Him. But He did rise on the third day and re-conquered. So, the last word of the Catholic or Christian is Christ is risen and He will conquer."

Hildebrand said to the bishops of the United States, "Go on your knees and pray and make sacrifices and ask God for the gift of faith for realizing in many ways you have failed your sheep."

When Steve Mosher was asked what message he would give the American bishops if he were given the opportunity, he said his message would be that "there is no priest shortage in the dioceses, which are led by bishops who preach the fullness of the truths of the Catholic faith.

"We have actually done studies in those dioceses where there is a willingness—a courageous willingness—to speak about the biblical/moral issues of our day. To speak about premarital sex and why it's wrong, to speak about the need to practice chastity

50

both before and after marriage, to speak about the fact that homosexuality is a grave sin."

Mosher said, "Those bishops who are preaching on this issue have no shortage of young men who are brought by the Holy Spirit to them, to join them in their teaching ministry."

Chapter 7

Why *Time* Magazine Must Be Fought to End the Catholic Scandal

The mother of all battles in the sex abuse wars was set for June 13–15, 2002, when the U.S. Conference of Catholic Bishops met in Dallas to enact measures to end the Catholic Church's sex scandal.

The media war had already begun, with *Time* magazine, in its Time-Life Building at Rockefeller Center in New York City, looking down on its opponents, led by *The Catholic World Report* magazine (*CWR*), located in a small building in the enemy's heartland, San Francisco.

Time fired the first shot with its May 20, 2002, article "Inside the Church's Closet: Gay priests talk about their hidden lives, love of the church and fear of being scapegoated in the sex scandals." *CWR* shot back with its May issue piece "Attitudes That Must Die: If the American bishops do not know how to respond to a public scandal, the laity must lead the way."

Time, allied with the gay movement, did a preemptive attack on what it called "[o]ne of the few concrete decisions the U.S. Cardinals made following their meeting in Rome with the Pope last month...to dispatch a team, called an apostolic visitation, to inspect all the nation's 220 seminaries and other preparatory institutions."

In what seemed an attempt to give marching orders on the strategic spin, *Time* almost immediately gave the rights to print the article to the Gay & Lesbian Alliance Against Defamation (GLAAD) website. The spin in the article was to call the apostolic visitation to the U.S. seminaries a "witch hunt."

According to the New York–based magazine's article, the inspection's purpose was "to determine whether the schools have been upholding orthodox moral doctrine in their applications process and in their classrooms.... Details about the visitation won't be worked out until the June 13–15 meeting of U.S. bishops in Dallas, according to a spokesman for the U.S. Conference of Catholic Bishops."

Time's solution to the Catholic Church's scandal was not "upholding orthodox moral doctrine" in the seminaries against sex abuse, but teaching "open dialogue." The director of St. Patrick's seminary in Menlo Park, California, the liberal Rev. Gerald Coleman, said that "psychosexual education and open dialogue are among the best ways to prevent inappropriate sexual behavior."

This open-dialogue approach to sex abuse prevention was even described. *Time* said, "At a recent meeting of Coleman's elective class, Homosexuality and the Church, words and phrases like penis, Freud, male rectum and 'Will & Grace' are bandied about without embarrassment."

(The Latin word 'rectum' means the intestine ending in the anus, the opening at the lower end of the alimentary canal for excretion. It is strange that a sex prevention class would discuss the place where homosexual intercourse occurs.)

Time Promotes Open Dialogue on Sex Abuse

According to talk radio host Bob Enyart's website, this is not the first time that *Time* has promoted open dialogue. Enyart wrote, "They [*Time*] printed a puff image piece on Peter Melzer, the editor of NAMBLA's journal. In the article 'For the Love of Kids' (November 1, 1993, page 51) the ACLU defended this pervert, arguing that if we condemn 'NAMBLA today, who is it tomorrow?' Melzer is also a New York City public school teacher (surprised?). He published an article 'In Praise of the Penises,' on 'how to make that special boy feel good.' As to a police report on Melzer's alleged sex with a Filipino boy, according to *Time*, there is no hard evidence that he abused this 'or any other boy in the U.S.'"

NAMBLA stands for the North American Man/Boy Love Association, whose slogan, according to Enyart, is "Sex by eight or it's too late."

The gay movement's foremost publication, *The Advocate*, which interviewed Bill Clinton in 1996, also promoted NAMBLA's position in an article titled "Getting Over It" on May 5, 1992, page 85. Enyart said, "Carl Maves wrote, 'How many gay men, I wonder, would have missed out on a valuable, liberating experience, one that initiated them into their sexuality, if it weren't for so-called molestation?'"

[http://www.enyart.com/features/writings/closet.shtml]

Both *Time* and the gays' foremost publication have had open dialogue on child molestation. With its own recent history of open dialogue about sex abuse, *Time* had the nerve to make a statement questioning the Church's account of the reasons for the sex abuse scandal.

The New York–based magazine's statement was contradictory. The article said, "Since many [most] of the victims are teenage boys, the [Church's] thinking goes, the perpetrators [male priests] must be gay—and that must be the problem, not sexual repression, not leaders who ignore serious criminal allegations."

Time's logic can only lead to two conclusions it didn't intend—one ridiculous and the other to the point. Either heterosexual priests are only pretending to be homosexuals when they commit homosexual acts on teenage boys, or homosexuality is an objective disorder like alcoholism, which can be treated, so even though one commits homosexual acts, one is not to be identified with a treatable disorder.

The logic gets even thinner when the article says that the reason for the sex abuse is sexual repression. The last thing *Time* magazine or anyone else could accuse Boston serial sex abuser Fr. Paul Shanley of is that he controlled, checked or suppressed his sexuality.

The *Worcester Telegram & Gazette* on April 9, 2002, published an article by The Associated Press that said: "In 1977, a woman from Rochester, N.Y., sent a letter to [then bishop of Boston] Medeiros with a summary of a meeting about homosexuality that Shanley attended. The summary quoted Shanley as saying he could 'think of no sexual act that causes psychic damage—not even incest or bestiality.'"

Time's One Valid Statement

Shanley is an example of the one valid statement in *Time*'s explanation of the reasons for the scandal. The fact is that Church leaders did "ignore serious criminal allegations."

Lawyer Roderick MacLeish said that documents proved that Cardinal Law of the Boston Archdiocese knew of Shanley's sex abuse and rape behavior since 1985, but the cardinal paid tribute to him in a 1996 letter for his "years of generous and zealous care" and said "you are truly appreciated." MacLeish said there had been 10 detailed complaints in Church documents and at least 26 complaints altogether filed against Shanley. ("Papers Outline Church Cover-up of Abuse Allegations," NewsMax.com, April 9, 2002) [http://www.newsmax.com/archives/articles/2002/4/8/183153.shtml]

The orthodox Catholic editor of *The Catholic World Report* (*CWR*), Phillip Lawler, agreed with *Time* magazine that Church leaders ignored sex abuse. In the editorial "Attitudes that Must Die," he said, "…many bishops behave as if clerics had special rights. Far too often, Church leaders and chancery aides defended the interest of the clerical fraternity rather than the Christian community."

CWR and *Time* also agreed that there is a high percentage of homosexuals in the priesthood. *Time* said that "the proportion [estimates from 15 percent to more than 50 percent] is higher than that of gay men in the male population at large," while *CWR* contended that even the lowest estimates of no higher than "the population in society at large" represent a "profound crisis."

CWR addressed "An Open Letter" on this crisis to the U.S. bishops who met in Dallas. The letter said: "In many ways the tepid response [of Church leaders] has been more scandalous than the abuse itself.... [E]vidence makes it impossible to ignore the widespread acceptance of homosexual activity among American priests.... [This] is a grave problem in itself because it causes disdain for Catholic doctrine and fosters a climate of hypocrisy among those who are the official representatives of Church teaching."

Time's Spin Is Opposite of Truth

However, while *Time*—which, remember, had open dialogue with the North American Man/Boy Love Association—appears to think that open dialogue, psychosexual education and ending sexual repression is the way to end the scandal, *CWR* as early as the year 2000 squarely stated that the problem is Church leaders "tolerating" the sin called "sodomy."

Fr. Paul Shaughnessy, in the November 2000 issue of *CWR*, wrote, "But everyone familiar with the current reality knows that the 'workshops on sexuality' offered [by 'politicized' psychologists] to priests and seminarians do not concern themselves with techniques helpful to self-mastery. Rather they take the form of group sharing sessions in which the participants are invited to make peace with their own 'sexuality' and urged [by psychologists], much more forcefully, to tolerate those with non-standard appetites.

Shaughnessy, more to the point, continued:

"The gay priest problem will continue to worsen as long as this code-talk remains the dominant idiom. As long as seminarians are 'educated in sexuality' by the Michael Petersons [a homosexual psychologist with a gay agenda]..., we can be sure that the number of gays will steadily increase in the clergy and the language of moral integrity will be pushed out of the discussion. Quite simply, those entrusted to fix what is broken are broken themselves and are camouflaging their real motives in the fuzzy vocabulary of therapy and pastoral sensitivity."

"I am not counseling disobedience or disrespect to bishops, and I am not denying that religious orders, even corrupt ones, are capable of working for the good of souls. But let's face facts. When more of your priests die by sodomy than by martyrdom, you know you've got a problem; when the man you bring in for the fix comes down with AIDS, you know you've got a crisis; and when the Pope first gets the facts thanks to *60 Minutes*, you know you're corrupt."

Can Liberal Church Leaders Act with Authority?

Liberal and so-called moderate bishops sometimes say they can't act with authority and mandate that orthodox Catholic moral doctrine be taught, let alone be practiced, in the seminaries.

CWR knows it is true that Church leaders can act with authority, because the magazine's publisher, Fr. Joseph Fessio, S. J., was exiled by the Jesuit Order. He was exiled after he criticized immoral and liberal teachings at the University of San Francisco (USF), including a play promoting sex abuse.

In the middle of the sex abuse scandal coverage on April 23, 2002, the *San Jose Mercury News* reported that Fessio, despite being America's top orthodox publisher of Roman Catholic literature, "has been forced into an obscure chaplain's job in Los Angeles after he criticized the University of San Francisco as too liberal and sought to open his own orthodox college." (Fr. Fessio has since been named chancellor of Ave Maria University in Michigan.)

Even though Fessio, 61 years old, has close ties with Cardinal Joseph Ratzinger, one of the pope's chief advisers, he was unable to stop the move, which took place in May 2002. He said, "They are trying to get me out of the way. Why else would they exile me? I am highly educated. I'm in the prime of my life. I have so much more to contribute than to minister to the sick."

The California Province of the Society of Jesus in Los Gatos—which was in the middle of its own sex scandal—refused to comment on the rationale for his displacement. But, according to the *Mercury News*, a former Catholic seminarian said, "They see him as a great threat to their agenda, which is to basically change the Church into another world order concept, a much more liberal one."

The forced exile has moral implications for faithful Catholics that have ironically been overshadowed by the sexual abuse scandal. The *Mercury News* mentioned that one of the main reasons for the exile was a "long-running criticism" of USF, a Jesuit-run school, by Fessio, the head of Ignatius Press.

One criticism he made in February 2002—just before his enforced exile—was about the USF establishment's plan to allow students to enact a production of the play *The Vagina Monologues*.

USF spokesman Gary McDonald, in defense of the production and open dialogue, said, "It is part of the job of a university to allow students to explore a range of issues and ideas.... It's not against the faith."

Fessio responded: "If UC-Berkeley wants to put on *Vagina Monologues*, that's OK. But a Catholic university doing that during Lent, the holy season, that's not a Catholic thing to do."

E. Michael Jones wrote in the April 2002 *Culture Wars* magazine that *The Vagina Monologues* is a sex abuse play. Commenting on the play when it ran at Notre Dame University, he said, "It also features a graphic description of the lesbian seduction of a minor, which is excused precisely because a lesbian is doing the molesting."

"Notre Dame University defended the performance precisely on the grounds of academic freedom; the bishop does nothing to contradict this undermining of morals," Jones said, "and in fact, in a scenario which has by now become familiar, those who attempt to defend the moral standard get punished."

Jones contends that liberals as well as those who cooperate with them in the Church are "culpable" because of "ineffective resistance to the dominant culture," while Fessio just wants to be left alone to teach the orthodox moral and faith teachings of the Church, including those against sex abuse.

"I don't think they're trying to make me suffer," Fessio said of his superiors. "But what I was trying to do with Campion College was offensive. They probably saw it as an implicit indictment of them. I just wish they would really allow a diversity of voices, including ours." (April 23, 2002, *San Jose Mercury News*)

In the May 2002 issue of Fessio's *CWR*, Theron C. Bowers Jr., M.D., said, "As a psychiatrist, I have a not-so-tongue-in-cheek strategy for clearing up the scandal. We could hypnotize the bishops into believing that these sexual offenders are orthodox, pre–Vatican II troglodytes."

Bowers hits on a truth that the U.S. bishops seem not to be getting. Faithful Catholics are losing faith in their bishops. Unfortunately, the bishops seem to care more about what the media think about them than the convictions of orthodox Catholics.

Chapter 8

Why the Soviet Republics of CBS, ABC and NBC's Suppression of Free Speech Must Be Fought to End the Church Scandal

CBS insider Bernard Goldberg, in his book *Bias*, compared the "media elite" to the "old Soviet Union" dictators as well as to Mafia bosses. The "News Mafia," as Goldberg calls the media, let its "reporters" know that the regime will not allow dissidence against its ally the gay movement. The crackdown on dissenters during the height of the Catholic scandal was regional, national, and international:

- Sam Donaldson and Cokie Roberts shouted George Will down on ABC's *This Week* when he tried to explain that the vast majority of priest sexual abusers are homosexuals. NewsMax writer Phil Brennan said, "After three or four attempts to get a word in edgewise, Will gave up." ("Isn't It Time for a Backlash?" NewsMax.com, June 19, 2002) [http://www.newsmax.com/archives/articles/2002/6/18/171550.shtml]

- Pope John Paul II's spokesman Dr. Joaquin Navarro-Valls in Rome was "greeted with a wave of protest." The *Jewish World Review* said Navarro-Valls received this greeting because he made the "link between homosexuality and sexual abuse by priests."

- Covering the Dallas bishops' sex abuse conference, *National Review*'s online preview of its July 1, 2002, issue said, "I'm hearing from inside press circles that reporters, editors and producers don't want to look at the gay issue. Michael S. Rose, author of *Goodbye, Good Men* [a book on homosexual abuses within the church] is in Dallas. I spoke yesterday to a TV reporter who wants to interview Rose about his findings, but who received word from the top to stay away from him."

These are only a few cases of the mass media's official suppression of the widely known fact that the vast majority of sex abusers are homosexuals. Cokie, Sam and their media accomplices are enforcing censorship that echoes memories of Soviet Russia and Nazi Germany.

Media Bias at Dallas Bishop Meetings

To get news at the time of the Dallas bishops meeting, reporters had to enter the underground world of homosexual spin organizations through their websites. For example, on June 15, the homosexual "information" group Gay & Lesbian Alliance Against Defamation (GLAAD) through its moles in the church reported news that the mass media censored.

Homosexual activist Cathy Renna, writing for GLAAD's website, said:

"We also learned more late last night about the anti-gay proposal offered by Bishop Fabian Bruskewitz of Lincoln, Neb. Bruskewitz's "Amendment 27" would have stated that because the "current homosexual culture" was the root cause of the sex abuse crisis, the bishops would be required to force strict conformity with all church doctrines on sexuality. His proposal was soundly rejected on a voice vote, with a source inside the meeting telling me that it received only perhaps a half-dozen votes of support."

During a victory get-together, Renna said, she met with "a number of familiar media faces" and Anne Barrett Doyle of the Coalition of Concerned Catholics, who is a member of the steering committee for the lay reform movement Voice of the Faithful.

According to Renna, "Anne was one of the first people I spoke with back in March when we were cultivating resources and contacts to offer media outlets.... Seeing Anne at the cathedral brought to mind how far we've come in the past months."

During those months, Cokie, Sam and the "News Mafia" had censored George Will, Pope John Paul II's spokesman, and the almost all conservative spokespersons in Dallas who attempted to report the "link between homosexuality and sexual abuse by priests," which *U.S. News & World Report* detailed before the crackdown.

(To be fair, the crackdown had a momentary lapse when Fox News host Brit Hume drolly said that allowing sex-abusing priests to marry wouldn't help "unless you let them marry men or little boys.")

But for the most part, only gay-approved "Catholic" lay reform activists like Anne Barrett Doyle, who together with the gay movement worked for months cultivating "resources and contacts to offer media outlets," were allowed to fully present their political agenda as "news" at Dallas.

'Catholic' Lay Reform Activists

Not to be outdone by the gay movement's GLAAD, *Time* magazine, in its June 17, 2002, issue, had its own "Catholic" lay reform activist, Mary Jo Bane, come forward to help the Church in its time of need. Bane said to *Time* that her "Catholic" lay organization and "power" plans were not "radical."

However, according to attorney Gregory A. Hession, president of Family Legal Services, Bane is a radical. He said on his website:

"They hate family autonomy, parental authority, home schoolers, and church authority.

"This is not an exaggeration. Dr. Mary Jo Bane, [former president] Clinton's Assistant Secretary of Administration for Children and Families in the Department of Health and Human Services, said, 'If we want to talk about equality of opportunity for children, then the fact that children are raised in families means there's no equality.... In order to raise children with equality, we must take them away from families and communally raise them.' Her federal department is in charge of the national effort to mold state DSS [Department of Social Services] departments into their image.

"That is what the communists believe. The following statement issued at a congress of Russian Communist Party educators in 1918 sounds like the credo of the modern DSS agent."
[http://www.massoutrage.com/dssdirtytricks.htm]

This Clintonian bureaucratic mindset is probably why the media and certain bishops are promoting Bane's Hillary-like governmental ideas of centralized takeover of church and family autonomy and authority. The bishops in Dallas created an Office for Child and Youth Protection to promote "safe environments" for children. Some have noted that so-called governmental "safe schools" and "safe spaces" are used by gay activists to promote homosexual agendas.

Some have joked that this is "an extension of the full employment act for homosexual and liberal Church bureaucrats." Some wonder if this is not another way to attack the very ones who for two decades have been fighting against homosexual sex abuse and other abuses in the Church—that is, the faithful orthodox Catholic laity and priests.

State Child Protection Services, under federal DSS agents, are notorious for taking children away from parents without any proof or due process and usually with only anonymous accusations. With the homosexual network inside the Church called the "Lavender Mafia" in control of many diocese bureaucracies, will orthodox laity and priests be targeted while homosexual sex abusers are protected by their gay allies?

Homosexual Network within the Church

Many believe that the homosexual network within the Church protected the gay sex abusers at the Dallas meeting. As the *National Review*'s Rod Dreher pointed out on June 13, 2002, "the need to avoid the 'elephant in the sacristy [the fact that the vast majority of priest sex abusers are homosexuals],' in Mary Eberstadt's memorable phrase, is perhaps the only point on which the bishops and the media agree."

To this end, the bishops running the Dallas meeting, according to the June 13 *National Review* article, had staged "briefings for the media on various aspects of the abuse scandal" by psychiatric panelists such as the Rev. Canice Connors, the Rev. Stephen Rossetti and others with a pro-homosexual agenda.

Connors is known among sex abuse victims for his psychiatric and "spiritual assessment" of mass pedophile Fr. John Geoghan. He wrote that "there are no particular recommendations concerning his spiritual life since he is involved in spiritual direction and seems to have a good prayer life."

While accepting psychiatric advice from the likes of Connors, the bishops in control of the meeting, however, refused the expertise of Catholic Medical Association (CMA) psychiatrists, who are faithful to the Church's full teachings. The CMA considered so-called expert Rossetti's advice to bishops as having helped create the sex abuse problem.

National Review's Dreher said, "The Rev. Stephen Rossetti, current president of St. Luke's,…is believed by some psychiatrists associated with the Catholic Medical Association to have been a big part of the problem, owing to the advice he's been giving bishops. Rossetti has most recently been downplaying the role homosexuality plays in the scandal."

American Psychiatric Association's 'Lavender Mafia'

The "Lavender Mafia" (the homosexual network within the Church) was probably the reason why CMA's psychiatrists were banned, wrote Dreher. According to psychiatrist Jeffrey Satinover, the American Psychiatric Association (APA) had its own "Lavender Mafia" when it voted to "normalize" homosexuality in the early 1970s.

The non-scientific as well as non-democratic Marxist and Nazi strategy used by the "Lavender Mafia" for its successful coup of the APA was explained by Satinover. The tactics used against the APA in the normalization of homosexuality are presented in his book *Homosexuality and the Politics of Truth*. Rep. Robert Dornan of California, on the floor of the House of Representatives, called the book "about the best book on homosexuality written in our lifetime." (See *Congressional Record*, May 8, 1996.)

Satinover said that "the leadership of a homosexual faction within the APA planned a 'systematic effort to disrupt the annual meetings of the American Psychiatric Association.' They defended this method of 'influence' on the grounds that the APA represented 'psychiatry as a social institution' rather than a scientific body or professional guild."

As one can clearly see, the "News Mafia" and the "Lavender Mafia" do not respect either freedom of speech or scientific bodies. They have created their own Iron Curtain, which is suppression of free speech.

The News Mafia–Lavender Mafia–Democratic Party Axis

The Berlin Wall was the symbol of Marxist ideology. Goldberg in his book *Bias* called ABC, NBC and CBS the three big "News Mafia" families. These "Big Three" are a large basis of the gay movement's power. The "News Mafia" is the New Berlin Wall that is even now starting to crumble, as did the Berlin Wall and the "evil empire" that build that wall.

Like Aleksandr Solzhenitsyn's *The Gulag Archipelago*, Goldberg's *Bias* is the beginning of the end for the new "evil empire." If talk radio and news sources like NewsMax continue to courageously fight the bias and lies of the "Big Three," then they will crumble as more and more viewers leave them.

But even the "Big Three" are only stooges of *The New York Times* and *The Washington Post*. Goldberg said, "The problem is that so many TV journalists simply don't know how to think about certain issues until *The New York Times* and *The Washington Post* tell them what to think. Those big, important newspapers set the agenda that network news people follow."

Fred Martinez

The gay movement appears to hold the "newspaper of record," *The New York Times*, in bondage in more ways than one. NewsMax ran an article about Accuracy in Media's Reed Irvine's inquiry into the *Times*' bias. Irvine said that *Times* national political correspondent Richard Berke spoke at a gathering of the National Lesbian and Gay Journalists Association.

Irvine said that Berke assured the homosexual group that the *Times* would remain very receptive to the gay agenda because "three-fourths of those who regularly attend the daily meetings that determine what will be on the front page of the *Times* the next morning are 'not-so-closeted' homosexuals."

Norman Mailer explains why this turning away from and rejection of natural objective truths such as heterosexual sex can lead to a Nietzschean state of affairs.

The non-Catholic Mailer's explanation needs to be repeated because he illustrates better than Catholics why their 20-centuries-old moral teaching that sex outside its natural purpose in a marriage between a man and a woman is sinful:

"So, yes, [homosexuals] in prison strive to become part of the male population, and indeed—it is the irony of homosexuality—try to take on the masculine powers of the man who enters them, even as the studs, if Genet is our accurate guide, become effeminate over the years.... Heterosexual sex with contraception is become by this logic a form of sexual currency closer to the homosexual than the heterosexual, a clearinghouse for power, a market for psychic power in which the stronger will use the weaker, and the female in the act, whether possessed of a vagina or phallus, will look to ingest or steal the masculine qualities of the dominator."

This totalitarian will to power and denial of natural objective truths may be the reason why Goldberg considered the media's anti-conservative bias against the great "social" issues such as abortion and homosexuality to be even greater than against the "Democrat-versus-Republican sort" of issues. He said, "Why were we doing PR for the AIDS lobby by spreading an epidemic of fear, telling our viewers about how AIDS was about to break out into mainstream heterosexual America, which simply was not true?"

But even in this there is a political dimension. Former Delaware governor Pete du Pont pointed out in a *Wall Street Journal* article after the 2000 Bush-Gore presidential race that when he compared maps, the adult video rental map and the map of the counties that went for Gore were the same.

E. Michael Jones, the editor of *Culture Wars* magazine, said in the February 2001 issue:

"If they want to survive as a party, the Republicans have to understand first of all, how sexual liberation is a form of political control, and secondly, how the Democrats increase their political power by mobilizing sexual deviance...things like pornography and its scholastic variant, sex education, in addition to abortion and homosexuality.... Those who are stupid enough to identify themselves with their sexual vices can always look to the Democratic Party and the dominant media culture as sympathetic to...guarantee his bondage."

Soviet Republics of CBS, ABC and NBC

The next battle in this war for freedom against the gay-media axis is again in the Catholic Church. The gay movement's spin organization, GLAAD, has already pointed to the next battle:

"With the Apostolic Visitations of U.S. seminaries expected to begin in August (and expected to last for two years), Dignity/USA and other church reform groups are going to be monitoring to see whether Vatican leaders will quietly attempt to purge gay men from the priesthood. GLAAD will be working closely with Dignity and our respective contacts inside the church to make sure the media are closely monitoring the process and outcomes of these visitations."

Time's May 20, 2002, issue in its preparation for the apostolic visitation of U.S. seminaries showed its strategy by using words like "hate" and "scapegoat" to color faithful Catholics and the Church's attempt to uphold its 2,000-year-old moral teachings in its own seminaries. The piece quoted a homosexual priest saying, "We're all sort of like Anne Frank's family, up in the attic, waiting for the Nazis to come."

This is the same Soviet-Clinton strategy used on CBS insider Goldberg after he wrote about bias in the media. The liberal Goldberg was ripped as a right-wing scoundrel by Dan Rather and other media elites, using words like "wacky charge," "weird," "bizarre" and "political activist" to discredit him and "divert attention" from the media elite's bias.

This is just another example of why the dominant media represent one of the last bastions of suppression of free speech within its own sovereign domain since the fall of the USSR. Goldberg was made, in his own words, a "nonperson" because he used his constitutional right of free speech to expose corruption in the Soviet Republics of CBS, ABC and NBC.

As liberal Goldberg said, "I was pointing fingers at the media elite, which only proved that I was the one who had a bias problem. Wasn't this what used to happen—on a much scarier and devastating scale, for sure—in the old Soviet Union? A dissident says the elite are corrupt, so the elite throw him in the Gulag because his accusations prove beyond any doubt...that the dissident is insane."

Media Elite's Soviet-Clinton Strategy against the Catholic Church

As in the case of Goldberg, the media elite's Soviet-Clinton strategy against the Catholic Church is false.

Its strategy of using words like "Nazis," "hate" and "scapegoat" to color faithful Catholics and the Church's attempt to uphold 20 centuries of moral teachings in its own seminaries is ridiculous.

It is also ironic, because the gay-media axis in fact used these Nazi-Marxist tactics against Goldberg and the American Psychiatric Association.

73

Fred Martinez

All persons who love freedom must be prepared to
monitor the gay-media axis' spin and tactics of
"influence" during the Vatican's apostolic visitation of
U.S. seminaries.

If faithful Catholics and the Vatican's attempt to
uphold its 2,000-year-old moral teachings in its own
seminaries can be terrorized by the same Marxist-Nazi
tactics used on the American Psychiatric Association
and Bernard Goldberg, what American organization or
person is safe?

Some Catholics think that the Vatican should send
an apostolic visitation not only to U.S. seminaries but
also to U.S. bishops.

Chapter 9

Why the Kinsey Lobby Advising the Bishops Must Be Fought for the Church Scandal to End

On August 21, 2002, *The Washington Times* reported that the U.S. Catholic bishops' sex abuse advisers are "people who have covered up...sex between men and children." Moreover, these advisers have had close association with "experts" who "defended sex between men and children."

"The bishops recently chose Dr. Paul McHugh, former chairman of the Department of Psychiatry and Behavioral Sciences at Johns Hopkins University School of Medicine, as chief behavioral scientist for their new clergy sex crimes review board," the Reisman-Jarrard report in the *Times* said.

"Yet Dr. McHugh once said Johns Hopkins' Sexual Disorders Clinic, which treats molesters, was justified in concealing multiple incidents of child rape and fondling to police, despite a state law requiring staffers to report them."

McHugh's subordinate, Johns Hopkins clinic head Fred Berlin, according to the report, "admitted he had covered for the sex criminals, angering legislators, child-advocacy groups and state officials. But his actions were not surprising, because 'at least eight men have been convicted of sexually abusing Maryland children while under [Berlin's] treatment there.'"

Fred Martinez

Dr. Judith Reisman and Dennis Jarrard, who wrote the report, are experts in the field of sex abuse and obscenity. Jarrard served as an adviser to the Los Angeles County Commission on Obscenity and Pornography, while Reisman is an internationally known expert on Alfred Kinsey and sex abuse.

Reisman is president of The Institute for Media Education and has been a consultant to three U.S. Department of Justice administrations and the U.S. Department of Education, as well as the U.S. Department of Health and Human Services.

Money Is Berlin's Mentor

The Reisman-Jarrard report said Berlin has been U.S. Catholic bishops' "chief adviser on child sexual abuse." Yet, according to Reisman, "Dr. Berlin described [pedophilia supporter] Dr. [John] Money as 'one of his most important mentors.'"

The Washington Times' report said, "Dr. Money once gave an interview to *PAIDIKA—the Journal of Paedophilia*, an 'academic' publication that advocates adult sex with children alongside ads for the North American Man/Boy Love Association (NAMBLA) and other pro-pedophilia groups. He told *PAIDIKA* that a 'relationship' that is 'totally mutual' between a boy of 10 or 11 and an adult male 'would not [be] pathological in any way.'"

On May 20, 2002, *The Wanderer*, a national Catholic weekly, said that the Money-Berlin advice to the bishops began when "the founder of the St. Luke Institute, Rev. Michael R. Peterson, M.D. (who later

76

died of AIDS), [urged] the Church to rely on Berlin and Money in a 1985 paper."

Money Is a Disciple of Kinsey

Reisman, quoted in the *Wanderer* article, said that "Dr. Berlin and John Money, Ph.D., co-founded a celebrated sexual training and treatment center, The Johns Hopkins Sexual Disorders Clinic.... Dr. Money, as it turns out, was a dedicated Kinsey disciple, the mentor for June Reinisch (the third Kinsey Institute director) and on the advisory board of the Kinsey Institute."

Another *Wanderer* piece on June 30, 2002, titled "The Real Experts Advise Bishops: Sue your Experts," claims much of the Church's "recent difficulties" have come about because "many of the Church's key sexuality advisors are associated with" the agenda created by Dr. Alfred Kinsey and the Kinsey Institute at Indiana University.

In the article, Reisman urges U.S. bishops to sue their Kinsey experts for malpractice:

"To me, this is a case of massive medical malpractice by those in the human sexuality field, as well as consumer fraud, as well as a broad spectrum of other things for the lawyers to sort out.... [T]hese so-called 'human sexuality educators' have been teaching behaviors that cause dysfunction, that are anti-authority and anti-Church."

The May 20 *Wanderer* article, by Paul Likoudis, said that "Kinsey and his colleagues were the driving force behind the legalization of fornication, adultery, bestiality, pedophilia and other immoral, harmful behaviors."

Fraudulent Scientific Data Eliminates Penalties for Sexual Offenses

Kinsey, because of the worldwide influence of his fraudulent scientific data, has been called the father of the homosexual movement by homosexuals, and the father of the sexual revolution as well as the pornography industry and the sex abuse lobby.

James H. Jones, an Indiana University scholar and Kinsey Institute insider, in an exposé biography titled *Alfred C. Kinsey: A Public/Private Life*, shows the motivation behind the Kinseyan "pan-sexualism" agenda.

In the report "How Junk Sex Science Created a Paradigm Shift in Society, Legislation and the Judiciary," Reisman said:

"Jones' data confirms other reports that Kinsey was a sexist, racist and atheist who excluded women, Jews, blacks, and moral traditionalists from his staff and hired only homosexuals and bisexuals (with one short-term exception). Kinsey only hired sexual deviants on whom he could rely to keep his secrets—including his [scientific] fraud, his "uncommon desires," and the child molesters he used to conduct child sex experiments. Jones also reported that Kinsey: coerced his wife into participating in acts of adultery and sodomy with his staff and co-authors (which were filmed), seduced male students at Indiana University (and bullied their wives into participating), filmed sex with his male co-workers (who were rewarded by promotion to co-authorship), and filmed himself participating in sado-masochistic sex rituals."

Reisman further showed how the Kinseyan sex abuse lobby worked when she stated: "Based on his [fraudulent scientific] data, Kinsey claimed that children enjoyed sex and the real harm of adult-child sex stemmed from 'hysterical' parents, teachers and professionals who reacted with anger and horror to children's disclosures. Based on his findings, many legislatures lightened or eliminated penalties for sexual offenses…toward children as 'victims' in cases of incest and child molestation."

In 1991, the widely respected British medical journal *The Lancet* verified Reisman's research when it demanded that the Kinsey Institute be investigated, writing:

"The Kinsey reports (one in 1948 on males and the companion five years later) claimed that sexual activity began much earlier in life…and displayed less horror of age differences and same-sex relationships than anyone at the time imagined. It was as if, to follow Mr. Porter again, 'Anything goes'. In [the book] *Kinsey, Sex and Fraud*, Dr. Judith A. Reisman and her colleagues demolish the foundations of the two [Kinsey] reports."

The Bishops, the 'Sex Experts' and the Media's Cover-Up

It is commonly believed that Kinseyan experts, such as Fred Berlin, Fr. Stephen Rossetti, Fr. Canice

Fred Martinez

Connors and others with a pro-gay agenda, in advising the Church leaders protected the gay sex abusers at the Dallas meeting.

The bishops, the Kinseyan "experts" and the mass media's suppression of the widely known fact that the vast majority of sex abusers in the Church scandal are gay was even contradicted earlier in the year, as stated before, by liberal columnists.

As stated earlier, *U.S. News & World Report* columnist John Leo said, "Most sexual victims of priests are teenage boys [abused in homosexual acts], according to one estimate. A study of Chicago's 2,200 priests identified 40 sexual abusers, only one of whom was a pedophile."

Also, Hastings Wyman, syndicated homosexual columnist, wrote: "[T]he pattern of sexual abuse among Catholic clergy does suggest a gay problem...90 percent of the cases of sex with adolescents that have come to light in the Church involved teenage boys, not girls. Do the math." (*Between the Lines*, May 22, 2002)

[http://www.rcf.org/pdfs/ProtectChildrenad.pdf]

During the Dallas bishops meeting on June 15, 2002, the homosexual spin group Gay & Lesbian Alliance Against Defamation (GLAAD) through its network in the Church reported news that the mass media censored.

As stated before, homosexual activist Cathy Renna, writing for GLAAD's website, said that liberal bishops within the church protected the gay sex abusers at the Dallas meeting: "We also learned more late last night about the anti-gay proposal offered by Bishop Fabian

Bruskewitz of Lincoln, Neb.... [which] was soundly rejected on a voice vote, with a source inside the meeting telling me that it received only perhaps a half-dozen votes of support."

During this time, the height of the media coverage of the Catholic scandal, the mass media outlets, under the influence of gay activists like Renna and her friend Barrett Doyle of Voice of the Faithful, had censored George Will, Pope John Paul II's spokesman Dr. Joaquin Navarro-Valls, and the almost-all-conservative representatives in Dallas who attempted to report the link between homosexuality and sexual abuse by priests.

VOTF and the Doyle-Peterson-Mouton Report

Activist Anne Barrett Doyle and her organization Voice of the Faithful (VOTF) have also taken part in the cover-up of the link between homosexuality and sexual abuse by priests.

In fact, VOTF has been promoting the 1985 report by Fr. Michael R. Peterson, which brought the Kinsey experts and pan-sexualism's non-"judgmentalism" into the Church.

As stated earlier, *The Wanderer* said that the Kinseyan advice to the bishops began when Peterson, who founded the St. Luke Institute (which Dallas panelists Connors and Rossetti later ran), urged "the Church to rely on Berlin and [pedophilia supporter] Money in a 1985 paper" and on his "pan-sexualism" at the St. Luke Institute.

Even the pro-gay *National Catholic Reporter*, on May 17, 2002, admitted: "The [Church's highest court, the Vatican] Signatura's brief, later published in the *Pittsburgh Post-Gazette*, stated: "St. Luke Institute [where the U.S. bishops send sex abuse priests], a clinic founded by a priest [Fr. Michael Peterson] who is openly homosexual and based on a mixed doctrine of Freudian pan-sexualism and behaviorism, is surely not a suitable institution apt to judge rightly about the beliefs and the lifestyle of a Catholic priest."

The liberal bishops continued to rely on Peterson for advice despite the Vatican's warning, as shown in the *National Catholic Reporter*'s May 17 article:

"By the time of Peterson's death [of AIDS], Cardinal James Hickey of Washington had come to rely on Peterson, along with a number of bishops, for advice in handling sex-offending members of the clergy. During the Mass, Hickey praised Peterson's work at St. Luke Institute, calling him a 'brilliant and hard-working priest.'"

According to the May 20 article in *The Wanderer* titled "The Homosexual Network and the 1985 Clergy Sex Abuse Report," Peterson was a "disciple" of John Money.

The 1985 Peterson report, which VOTF has been promoting, said:

"We have been hampered in our profession by extreme moral judgmentalism, if I may use the phrase, and it is only in very few medical schools in this country that the issue is treated or even addressed properly. The Johns Hopkins Hospital Sexual Disorders Clinic run by Dr. John Money [who became a pedophilia supporter] and Dr. Fred Berlin [who later covered up for the sex criminals] is probably the 'authority' scientific community. I know personally both of these highly respected scientists and I am very appreciative of their efforts to bring this psychiatric disorder out of the shadows and into the 'scientific daylight' so that we can begin to see the disorder as a psychiatric disease and not a moral weakness." [http://alterboys.tripod.com/moutonreport/Page_1x.html]

The VOTF website said that the winner of its first VOTF Priest of Integrity Award, the Rev. Thomas Doyle, "[joined] with Rev. Michael Peterson, a priest/psychiatrist who founded a treatment center for clergy, and Ray Mouton, a Louisiana lawyer, [to write] a comprehensive report in 1985, and sent it to every bishop, identifying sexual abuse as a compulsive, lifelong psychosexual disorder, not a moral weakness."

In a report found on the Survivors Network of those Abused by Priests (SNAP) website called "A Short History of the Manual," Doyle said that Money's disciple Peterson "was a friend and collaborator." The "Short History" report said the manual was an "instrument about how to deal with cases of priest-pedophilia." [http://www.snapnetwork.org/]

However, the manual failed to bring out that the homosexual sex abuse of teenage boys is the overwhelmingly largest component of the problem, which then as now is 90 percent or more of the Catholic sex abuse scandal. Also, in the case of Catholic priest pedophilia abuse, the vast majority are boys.

Even the Doyle-Peterson-Mouton manual said, "In my experience, most of the pedophiliac clerics I have seen and my colleagues have dealt with are homosexual pedophiles and not heterosexual pedophiles; this is surprising since the greater percentage in the general population is the opposite."

But instead of bringing out the homosexual abuse problem as the main portion of the scandal, the manual calls it a "Compulsive Heterosexual/Homosexual Acting Out," "Pedophilia or Sexual Molestation of Minors" and "Exhibitionism" problem.

The Doyle-Peterson-Mouton manual said—and Bill Clinton would appreciate this—that "exposing the genitals" to unfamiliar persons "represents one of the 'victimless crimes.'"

But the main problem is that the manual uses the standard gay activist spin that VOTF's Anne Barrett Doyle, GLAAD and the media used to censor conservatives in Dallas who attempted to report the link between homosexuality and sexual abuse by priests.

The tactic, as Peterson used for the most part in the Executive Summary of the manual, is to say that the scandal is about pedophilia and then claim that pedophilia is not associated with homosexuality, but is a heterosexual problem or at most a heterosexual/homosexual problem.

The gay activist expert and psychiatrist Jeffrey Satinover, who wrote the book *Homosexuality and the Politics of Truth* (cited by California representative Robert Dornan on the floor of the House of Representatives as "about the best book on homosexuality written in our lifetime" (*Congressional Record*, May 8, 1996), states this is a standard spin:

"Activists are aware of the adverse effect on the gay-rights movement that could result if people perceived any degree of routine association between homosexuality and pedophilia…. They have denied this association by focusing on the (true) fact that—in absolute numbers—heterosexuals commit more child molestation than homosexuals."

"But careful studies show that pedophilia is far more common among homosexuals than heterosexuals."

According to an article by correspondent Ellen Rossini, "'Although heterosexuals outnumber homosexuals by a ratio of at least 20 to 1, homosexual pedophiles commit about one-third of the total number of child sex offenses,' said Tim Dailey, a senior fellow for culture studies at the Family Research Council." (The National Catholic Register, September 15–21, 2002)

[http://www.ncregister.com/Register_News/091002sem.htm]

From the information that Kinsey expert Reisman has documented, Peterson was only following the Kinseyan advice of his mentors Money and Berlin, until his death of AIDS in 1987. Also, Peterson, who was homosexual—as with the gay Kinsey in his data—probably felt a need to cover up the gay connection to the scandal in order to protect his gay subculture.

Fred Martinez

Doyle and VOTF Have No Excuse

But Fr. Doyle and VOTF, which is the mass media's favorite "Catholic" lay organization to cure the Catholic Church of its sex abuse scandal, have no excuse.

Every knowledgeable person without an agenda knows the fact that at least 90 percent of the problem is homosexuals "acting out" on teenage boys. VOTF and Doyle have failed to bring out this fact in their many media opportunities.

In fact, in the 1996 Doyle-Demarest memo, Doyle uses the gay activist spin:

"In the past it was common to refer to priests who had sexually abused male children as homosexuals when in fact 'pedophiles' would have been the correct term.... I am convinced that the use of the term "homosexual" when referring to actions with young boys actually meant pedophilia or at least pedophilic acts."

Some orthodox Catholics wonder why VOTF, if it really wants to end the sex abuse scandal, gave the Priest of Integrity Award to Doyle instead of to the Latino Fr. Enrique Rueda, who in 1982 wrote *The Homosexual Network: Private Lives and Public Policy.*

In the book Rueda documented how disgraced homosexual archbishop Rembert Weakland and other Church leaders brought gay activists into the heart of the Church. Connie Marshner of the Free Congress Foundation wrote in a March 2002 article, "We Were Warned":

"The name of the fair city of Boston appears frequently in Fr. Rueda's pages, giving it the dubious distinction of being the birthplace of NAMBLA, the North American Man/Boy Love Association (an interesting coincidence in light of subsequent developments). Also interesting to note is that one [now infamous mass pedophile] Fr. Paul Shanley attended the NAMBLA convention in Boston, supposedly on behalf of the then-Catholic Archbishop, Medeiros."

"In the early days of 'gay liberation,' 1972, a National Coalition of Gay Organizations adopted a 'Gay Rights Platform.' This list of demands included one to repeal all laws governing the age of sexual consent—a matter of some obvious concern to pederasts."

For his efforts to end the scandal, Reuda, according to the March 30, 2002, *The Wanderer* article, was "exiled by his bishop Matthew Clark of Rochester, NY, refused incardination by every other American bishop, and is today an official 'nonperson' in the American church."

If VOTF and the liberal bishops really want to end the church scandal, then they have to stop covering up the gay part of 90 percent of the scandal. If VOTF and Doyle really want to end the pedophilia part of the scandal, then they have to expose the fraudulent scientific data eliminating penalties for sexual abusers and the Kinseyan "experts" who are advising the bishops.

If not, then VOTF needs to take the advice that Doyle gave in Canada in 2002:

Fred Martinez

"Any institution that enables the cover-up, protects the abusers or the authorities that hide them, doesn't deserve to exist."

Chapter 10

Who Is Responsible for the Catholic Scandal and What Is the Solution?

The New York Times and *The Boston Globe*, as well as newspapers in Ireland and on the European landmass, have been promoting Voice of the Faithful (VOTF) as having a solution to the Catholic Church's sex abuse scandal.

The VOTF solution to the scandal is to democratize the "authoritarian" Church and have the bishops cede authority to lay Catholics.

For this group, "democracy" appears to mean that the bishops should cede their authority to lay "Catholics" such as possibly pro-gay abortion advocates like Leon Panetta, Bill Clinton's former chief of staff, or Robert Bennett, who was Clinton's hardnosed lawyer in the Paula Jones sex scandal.

If that's the case, then VOTF is too late because the U.S. Conference of Catholic Bishops has already attempted to cede these Clintonian "sex abuse experts" authority on its 12-member National Review Board, created to deal with the sexual abuse scandals.

It's obvious that groups such as VOTF—which are calling for "democracy" because bishops are "tyrannical rulers"—don't know many bishops. The reason there is a crisis is because many bishops—far from being tyrants—cede or refuse to use their authority to discipline liberals who are abusing their positions to morally corrupt the Catholic people.

The problem is that many bishops are acting like politicians.

Even Frank Bruni in the October 20, 2002, *New York Times* admitted that "American Bishops were responding to the child sexual-abuse crisis in an almost secular, political fashion: rewriting rules, confessing faults and acknowledging that they need outsiders [such as Panetta and Bennett] to keep them honest."

Bishops as Politicians

Many bishops, instead of steadfastly upholding the moral teachings of Jesus Christ, act like politicians worrying about the media and liberal diocese bureaucrats. Thus the media and liberal bureaucrats control even many otherwise orthodox bishops by intimidation.

According to James Hitchcock, professor of history at St. Louis University:

"[I]n [a diocese] environment governed by ideology, this [orthodox] scenario really cannot play itself out. Liberals are quick to notice even small 'backward' steps by their bishop, and they test him by relentlessly pushing ahead with their agenda, so that he must either confront them or surrender."

Professor Hitchcock said in the May 1995 *Catholic World Report*, "Conservative secular journalists have cynically invented the 'Strange New Respect Award' which the media bestow on conservative public figures willing to betray their principles. Every bishop, whether or not he hankers after the award, knows that it exists.

"(Thus in one diocese a bishop with a national reputation for conservatism before he was appointed now enjoys regular encomia from the local media, even as he actively cooperates in portraying conservative Catholics as unbalanced fanatics.)"

Conservative bishops also find that the full moral teachings of the Church are undermined by their fellow bishops and that they are treated as second-class citizens for their orthodoxy. Hitchcock, who is a founder of the Fellowship of Catholic Scholars, said:

"Despite fifteen years of episcopal appointments by John Paul II, the National Conference of Catholic Bishops remained essentially a liberal body, in which determined conservatives have difficulty merely staving off serious defeats, much less winning substantial victories.

"Once again it requires a particularly resolute kind of man to accept the status of a defined minority within a body which seems to place great importance on the spirit of belonging.

"If nothing else, a new bishop is likely to discover quickly that he will be consistently on the losing side unless he moderates his positions substantially."

According to Hitchcock, the Vatican since 1980 has appointed bishops who are "personally orthodox and pious but low-keyed, cautious, and 'non-confrontational.'"

Unfortunately, through the 1970s the Holy See appointed liberal bishops who were "tolerant of dissent" as well as some who were "personally sympathetic" to dissent.

The problem is that the personally orthodox but non-confrontational weak bishops are profiled for failure when confronted by hardened doctrinaire liberals and, in some cases, hardened doctrinaire sexual revolutionaries with agendas.

Sexual Revolutionaries in the Church

Catholic journalist Paul Likoudis, in his book *Amchurch Comes Out: The U.S. Bishops, Pedophile Scandals and the Homosexual Agenda*, presents the case that sexual revolutionaries, although a small minority, are to some extent in control of the American Catholic Church.

Likoudis documents that since the 1950s many bishops' offices and other top management positions within the Church were filled by men of "perverse sexuality." These men created an Old Boy network with those of like mind to corrupt the sexual morality of Catholics in catechism and by sexual abuse.

Fr. Joseph Wilson, who wrote the foreword to *Amchurch Comes Out*, explains the bishop crisis in a nutshell in an article titled "The Coming-Out Party— Unpacking the Mystery":

"If you stop for a few moments and quietly ponder the fact that the percentage of bishops whose names have been linked with sexual incidents is appreciably larger than the percentage of priests, it begins to seem less mysterious that so many sexual offenders in the priesthood were tolerated by their bishops."

One central figure in the corruption of Catholic
sexual morality was Clinton's Cardinal, Joseph
Cardinal Berdardin. In appreciation for all he had done
for the cultural elites' sexual revolution, Berdardin, on
what Likoudis calls his "well-publicized death-bed,"
was visited by Hillary and received a letter from Bill
Clinton.

'The Most Influential Bishop in the History of America'

Likoudis calls Berdardin "the most influential
bishop in the history of America." Neither orthodox
Catholics nor liberal "Catholics" deny his influence.
Likoudis said:

"No one disputes his influence: as creator of the
National Conference of Catholic Bishops and the
United States Catholic Conference: as a bishop-maker
who...consoled and empowered dissenters while
professing his loyalty to his Roman superiors; as an
architect of proposals to deconstruct the Roman
liturgy, Catholic education and the all-important field
of catechetics."

What the liberal "Catholics" and the media have
covered up about "the most influential bishop in the
history of America," according to *Amchurch Comes
Out*, was that "one after another of Berdardin's closest
clerical friends from his native Diocese of Charleston
made the newspapers for charges of pedophilia: Fr.
Eugene Condon, Fr. Justin Goodwin, Fr. James Robert

Owen-Howard, Fr. F. X. Seitz, in addition to continuing allegations against [Monsignor Frederick] Hopping," a friend and seminary roommate of Berdardin.

Documenting not only that Berdardin's friends were involved in alleged sex abuse, Likoudis also shows that some of his closest bishop friends were in many ways "responsible" for the infamous Fr. Rudy Kos pedophile scandal of the Diocese of Dallas in the 1990s. *Amchurch Comes Out* said:

"As the trail involving Kos evolved, it was revealed that two of 'Berdardin's boys'—his closest friends in the episcopacy—Archbishop Thomas C. Kelly, OP, of Louisville and Archbishop Michael Sheehan of Santa Fe—were responsible."

Likoudis as well exposes a number of other lesser known bishops and Church leaders who were Berdardin clones. The thread that ties all these Church leaders together is their pro-gay advocacy and activism "to deconstruct the Roman liturgy, Catholic education and the all-important field of catechetics."

The reason for this activism is summed up by Fr. Wilson:

"If sexual autonomy is one's goal, one will not want the traditional Mass as the central symbol of the Faith, for the very form it takes will always seem a reproach.... And as for catechesis: well, why else would one promulgate religion textbooks that avoided subjects such as commandments, precepts of the Church, original sin; why else would one find situation ethics attractive—unless one were anxious to usher in a new religion, one much more amenable to one's whims."

Sexual Revolutionaries' New Religion

According to Likoudis, the doctrinaire liberals as well as the sexual revolutionaries in the Church, with their liturgical "reform," have caused a 60 percent decline in Mass attendance.

The liberals' catechetical and "tolerance" parochial school reform has led to two-thirds of Mass-going Catholics not being able to "identify the Catholic doctrine on the Eucharist" and eighth-graders who are "learning about anal sex and bestiality in their Catholic school classrooms," according to Fr. Wilson.

If what Likoudis and Wilson say is true, then the liberals have created a religion that is not Catholicism. The new religion appears to be pan-sexualism, in which original sin and personal sin are denied. Pan-sexualism in its extreme form allows all sexual acts, including homosexuality, anal sex, bestiality, and sexual abuse of children.

As shown earlier, according to the May 17, 2002, issue of the liberal *National Catholic Reporter*, the Vatican knows about pan-sexualism in the Church.

If some liberals are doctrinaire pan-sexualists, then they will pretend to promote policies against sexual abuse only as a means of public relations. However, they will, with the cover of the cultural elites' media, continue to promote and act out sexual perversions that are in opposition to 20 centuries of Catholic moral teachings.

The only change will be that the sexual revolutionaries will have to become cleverer in their war against Catholic morality. And, as seen in the case of Bill Clinton, if they stay true to doctrinaire pan-sexualism, then the media will cover up their sex scandals and protect them.

Orthodox Catholics' Two Choices

Orthodox Catholics have only two choices if it is true that such liberals and revolutionaries are in many of the Church's top leadership positions.

They can do nothing and, as a result, allow the liberals and revolutionaries to continue to corrupt the young people of the Church. In that case, in a few decades not even a third of the Catholics in the U.S. will know or support the most central Catholic moral and faith teachings.

Remember, liberal catechetical and parochial school "reforms" have made it possible for two-thirds of Mass-going Catholics to no longer be able to "identify the Catholic doctrine on the Eucharist."

In addition, even though the Catechism of the Catholic Church states that "homosexual acts are intrinsically disordered…[and] under no circumstances can they be approved," these same "reforms" have made it possible, as reported in recent polls, for 80 percent of high school seniors who are Catholic to believe (contrary to Church teaching) that homosexuals should have the "right" to marry, while around two-thirds of adults agree with the Church's position that gay marriages should not be legal, according to the September 6, 2001, *The Wanderer* newspaper.

If this trend continues, in three decades the vast majority of these Catholic high school seniors, who are the future Church and most of those "reformed" during these future decades by "Catholic" education, will cease to be Catholic.

The Catholic Church in America will increasingly cease to exist except for a few orthodox Catholic colleges, the Catholic homeschoolers and a few orthodox Catholic dioceses and parishes.

The other choice the people of the U.S. Church have is to first pray and then do everything under their power to influence the Vatican to start appointing a new type of bishop, one who is not afraid to confront sexual revolutionaries in the media as well as among his fellow bishops and bureaucrats.

These strong bishops—like good fathers—must be willing to discipline those who refuse to stop corrupting the Catholic youth. They must be willing to fire bureaucrats who refuse to abandon pan-sexualism. They must be willing to come under fire to the point of martyrdom from the pan-sexualist media and their liberal "Catholic" allies.

If the Vatican does not start appointing this new type of strong bishop, then Catholics in the United States must start joining orthodox Catholic parishes as well as groups such as the Apostolate for Consecration, the Legion of Mary and other groups like these that are loyal to the pope and to the full teachings of the Church.

(The real fruit of Vatican II and John Paul II are these young spirited groups, which, one hopes, will lead to the evangelization of America as the old "Catholic" liberals fail to replace themselves because they offer the young only secularism with a Catholic veneer.)

These young groups are protected by the Vatican and offer refuge as well as support to orthodox Catholic families whose faith is often literally under siege. Such groups must be rallied round to grow rapidly so that if the Vatican waits a few decades to reform the bishops of America, then there will still be a strong contingent of Catholics to enjoy the reform.

In other words, it will be the job of these groups to evangelize the Catholics who are being run through the liberal catechetical and "reformed" parochial school programs if the Vatican doesn't act.

Pope John Paul II Needs Prayers

But most importantly, Catholics must pray for Pope John Paul II and his successor.

Everyone must remember that, for whatever reason John Paul II has for not appointing strong bishops, both he and his office of Pope (the holder of the keys of Peter) are hated and seen as a last stronghold against the sexual revolutionaries.

In nation after nation, at the World Summit for Children, from Beijing to Cairo, he is one of the last worldwide bastions fighting against the cultural elite's agenda.

Remember, the timing of the media's "breaking" story was when John Paul II's health appeared to be deteriorating. The media in fact were sending correspondents to Rome with the expectation of a papal conclave.

On June 14, 2002, Mary Jo Anderson reported on the website WorldNetDaily:

"The [*Boston*] *Globe* and others have known for over a decade about the growing gay sub-culture in the Church, but the *Globe* and others simply winked—they are no less guilty of a cover-up than Cardinal Law. It did not seem worthy of print. Until, that is, Pope John Paul II, the disliked "reactionary" pope, faltered during Christmas masses."

According to Anderson, the goal of the timing of the scandal-reporting was "to create chaos" and to build "momentum" so that "the cardinals can be stampeded into electing an unusual pope: a candidate approved by *The New York Times* and the United Nations."

As can be seen, the pope and the office of Peter need prayers even as Catholics pray and work toward moving the Vatican to appoint strong bishops.

Orthodox Catholics should take heart because this may be a time when the Vatican, after seeing the U.S. bishops in politician mode, might be ready to listen to calls for strong orthodox bishops.

The Vatican may now be aware of the American bishops' confusion as to "who they are."

This newfound Roman awareness that bishops were acting as politicians instead of the successors of the Twelve Apostles of Jesus Christ was confirmed by an article in the October 20, 2002, *New York Times*. The article, by Frank Bruni, was titled "Vatican Defends Authority: U.S. [Bishops'] Sex-Abuse Policies that Cede Power to Lay People Rankle Rome."

According to the article, a Roman Church official said, "They're [U.S. bishops] dealing with the matter as if they don't understand who they are."

In his 2002 book *The Courage to be Catholic: Crisis, Reform, and the Future of the Church*, George Weigel said that because of archaic and poor information-gathering methods, the pope and the curia before the scandal had "a generally high impression of the U.S. hierarchy." But if *The New York Times* report is correct, then the crisis may have changed the Vatican's impression.

Vatican insider Weigel in his book indicated that Rome may be willing to listen to loyal orthodox Catholic input on how to fix the U.S. hierarchy.

Orthodox Catholics must take this change in the winds to heart in order to pray as well as do all in their power to help the pope and curia understand the need to appoint new bishops who act like the successors to the Twelve Apostles.

Section Three

Why Heroes Are Needed to End the Modern Nightmares We Face

Whether or not the Vatican fixes the U.S. hierarchy, Catholics and all persons who believe in the reality of God, love, beauty, free will and responsibility must make a choice.

Are they going to be like Spider-Man or Bill Clinton?

Only heroes can defeat the culture that Clinton in part helped to create. Only heroes can end the modern nightmares we all face. Toward this purpose Spider-Man can help us understand what a hero is.

Fred Martinez

Chapter 11

Heroes and Anti-heroes: Spider-Man vs. the Bill Clinton Culture

Steve Ditko, the original artist and co-creator of the *Spider-Man* comic, which is now a record-breaking hit movie, is the Greta Garbo of comic book artists.

Refusing to give interviews for the last 20 years, he recently refused interviews for major articles about him by the *Los Angeles Times* and one of Canada's leading newspapers, the *National Post*.

Ditko, however, did explain his philosophy of art in a narrative on a 1987 video titled *The Masters of Comic Book Art*, hosted by author Harlan Ellison. In his introduction, Ellison dismissed Ditko's plea that heroes in art and literature be measured by the moral courage shown in objective good-versus-evil choices.

The artist now seems prophetic for saying in the program that if we glorify the anti-hero in art, then anti-life and violence will come into our culture. The anti-heroes of the Columbine-like killings in public schools and the September 11 terrorists seem to justify his claim.

What our American and global culture needs are heroes as models. In the program, the artist and co-creator of Spider-Man says: "Aristotle said that art is more important than history. History tells how man did act. Art shows how man should and could act. It creates a model."

"The self-flawed and anti-hero provide the heroic label without the need to act better. A crooked cop, a flawed cop, is not a valid model of a good law enforcer," Ditko said in the program. "An anti-cop corrupts the legal good, and an anti-hero corrupts the moral good."

Spider-Man as a Model for Good

The power of Ditko's art has in fact influenced youth toward good. In the Fall 2001 issue of the online Jesuit magazine PARTNERS, a teenager named Pedro told how he was inspired to go to college by Spider-Man's message.
[http://www.jesuits-chi.org/contactmagazine/2001fall]

"Spider-Man got his power when he was a teenager and wasn't sure how to use it," Pedro explained. "So his grandfather [actually uncle] told him, 'With greater power comes greater responsibility.' That's the way it is at Cristo Rey. We're learning to make the world a better place. We're going to go to college and give a whole lot back from what we've been given."

Some are saying that Spider-Man is even a type of Christ. In his essay for the video, Ditko seems at times to be describing Spider-Man as well as Christ. He says, "Early comic book heroes were not about life as it is, but creation of how a man with a clear understanding of right and wrong and the moral courage to choose acts, even if branded an outlaw."

On the Internet, I found the testimony of a man who used Ditko's art to turn to God. Mark Dukes, now a deacon of the African Orthodox Church, said:

"My father wasn't around. My mother was a single parent. It was a vacuum in my life. Who am I supposed to be? How am I supposed to be?

"For me, Spider-Man really resonated. Spider-Man's alter ego was Peter Parker, who was a nerd. And I didn't feel like I was a cool guy either. Spider-Man was disliked and feared. Everyone thought he was a crook, but he was a good guy. No one gave him any respect but he continued to do good even in the face of all that.

"He would sacrifice himself, get beat up and then people would say 'Ahhh. Spider-Man! Run. He's going to do something to us!' And really he had just now saved the world. That is very saintly.

"For me, Spider-Man was a type of Christ. He went through suffering just to do good. And he continued to do it even in the face of everyone misunderstanding him and hating him."

Spider-Man, Icon Art and Invisible Realities

Dukes is an artist of Orthodox icons for churches, which is art that, like Ditko's early drawings of Spider-Man, has little perspective or photo-realistic graphics.

Blake Bell, creator of Ditko.Comics website, said:

"Visually, Ditko had what most people would consider a cartoony style, but his work was far more real than the "photo-realist" comic artists that would appear on the scene in the following 20 years.

"His was more real because the visual laws defined in his universe were so real, so consistent, that one suspends disbelief to its maximum."

Icon historian Andrei Navrozov, in the June 2002 issue of *Chronicles*, agrees with Bell that art can be about either "gaining a deeper understanding" of reality by symbols or "mimicking" reality.

Perspective was first invented in 470 B.C. by Agatharchus as a means of "geometric illusionism" to mimic reality in stage sets for the theater, according to Navrozov.

The icon historian said the "theater set is conceived as a fiction, whereas [an icon] painting is born as an attempt at truth of life, an attempt that in no sense compromises the integrity of the original [reality].... They are symbols of real life, not lifelike imitations of reality.

"There is no deeper conflict in history than that between these opposing views of art. 'Is art to serve reality and the individual under God or is it to serve [materialistic] realism and the masses under communism?"

Navrozov shows us that the modern battleground against God and reality is imagery and the imagination. Michael O' Brien said in *A Landscape with Dragons: The Battle for Your Child's Mind* that imagination is the way that mankind comprehends "God's territory" and his created "invisible realities."

The modern imagination, according to O'Brien, has lost "God's territory" by returning to its "pre-pagan split in consciousness," which is the Gnostic rejection of the "sacramental" unity of spirit and matter, the addiction to occult tales of will to power like Harry Potter, and the relativistic denial of good and evil with ends-justify-the-means storylines.

J. R. R. Tolkien's *The Lord of the Rings* is for O'Brien a prime example of a return to the Western Christian epic tradition of the moral imagination, which comprehends "God's territory" and his created "invisible realities."

O'Brien said, "The discernment of the right paths that must be taken, if good is to triumph, is dramatized in the myriad geographical, emotional, spiritual, and symbolic choices faced by the questers. In each of these, Tolkien's world is faithful to the moral order of the universe, to the absolute necessity of freedom. Middle-earth is a "sacramental" world, an "incarnational" world.... Spirit [invisible realities] and matter are never portrayed as adversaries."

Western Culture Based on Reality and God

The Western Christian culture was rooted in this service to reality and God. Reality was the belief in the objectivity of things both material and spiritual. During the last two to five centuries, materialistic modernity has been the adversary of this "incarnational" worldview, which encompasses both spirit and matter.

This "incarnational" reality was rooted out and replaced with a worldview of materialistic science and "realism" in art—in which reality was found only within material objects that could be tested and seen.

Spiritual (invisible) realities like God, love, beauty, responsibility and free will were neither material nor testable, so they were not within modernity's realism.

Modernity attacked the primacy of realistic philosophies such as Thomism and realistic symbolic literature, such as Dante's spiritual epics and Shakespeare's dramas, contrasting persons who were symbols of the conflicting worldviews of modernity and the older realistic philosophy.

Hamlet's "To be or not to be?" illustrates what the two cultures were in conflict about. In our time, Clinton ("What is the definition of 'is'?") is the symbol of modernity's denial of "to be," or objective truth or falsehood.

Modernity, in its desire to stamp out the Christian culture, dislodged Thomism realistic philosophy and realistic symbolic literatures with Pavlovian behaviorism as well as materialistic reductive studies and modern art, which represented only materiality. Examples are Freud's deterministic reduction of all symbols of the mind to represent only the physical acts of sex and Picasso's sexual anti-art.

This cramped reality of only the materially seeable or testable led to rootlessness and alienation, which was so unbearable to modern man that there was a reaction. According to philosophy professor Allan Bloom, Friedrich Nietzsche's philosophy of disbelief in all reality, seeable or unseeable—material or spiritual—became the language of the American reaction.

Nietzsche's values philosophy led to the subjectivity of all concepts of objective truth, which included good and evil.

Many will remember that when President Reagan called the USSR the "evil empire" he was roundly criticized for violating the new language of "beyond good and evil." This language of value relativism allows for neither the words nor the symbols of evil and good.

Nietzsche's anti-reality philosophy of "God is dead" led to the anti-heroes of politics and art.

In society this led to the denial of the concepts of absolute truth and the law of identity in reality by artists such as Pablo Picasso and by politicians such as Bill Clinton. This rejection of good and evil in turn led to the degrading of women and sexuality.

In the case of Picasso, E. Michael Jones in *Degenerate Moderns* says:

"His break with the traditions was an index of his hatred not only toward the spiritual values of the West but toward the human body and spirit that the West prized as good. In the end, the only thing that Picasso portrayed realistically was the woman's crotch. Modern art had returned to its roots, and the gaping crotch was the only thing now that could keep the aging Picasso in touch with the real world."

Spider-Man the Hero

On the other hand, the hit movie *Spider-Man* may be a sign that our society wants to return to the culture that Nietzsche, Picasso and Clinton rejected—a culture that was able to see the objective reality of God, love, beauty, responsibility, free will and the honorable hero.

In the movie's climax the Green Goblin stands at the top of a bridge holding in one hand the woman Spider-Man loves and in the other hand a cable with a tram full of children dangling at its end.

Fred Martinez

Then the villain releases both. As he does, he gives Spider-Man a choice: "You can save either the girl or the children."

Spider-Man, almost miraculously, saves both. For some, this scene is symbolic of the need in our society to return to the Christian tradition of men retaking the heroic responsibility of showing love by committing both to their women and to the fruit of their love through "better or worse" for life.

As our hero slowly lowers his love and the children to safety, the Green Goblin repeatedly attacks him.

The Goblin taunts him to let go and save himself, which would mean the deaths of those he is lowering to the ground. But as the villain zeros in for the kill, Spider-Man is ready to give his life for others, as another hero did 2,000 years ago.

With the help of New Yorkers on the bridge, Spider-Man saves his love and the children while defeating the Goblin, who finally begs for mercy. As our hero is apparently about to give the Green Goblin his hand, the villain sends his high-tech vehicle to kill Spider-Man from behind. Spidey avoids the vehicle and it ends up killing the Goblin.

This is the Christian message in a symbolic nutshell.

God will forgive anyone no matter what the offense, with only one exception. The only offense God can't forgive without destroying our free will is one's choice to reject mercy. By the Judas choice, one freely sends oneself to where God is not, which is the definition of hell.

Pornography and Clinton the Anti-Hero

The Democrats and their public relations agency, the media, are at the other end of the symbolic spectrum, as real-life anti-heroes who use the seduction marketing trick of association to sell lies.

Years ago, in Catholic books, association meant personal relationships with good or bad companions—friendships that led to depravity or honorable lives.

Association now means creating the false impression that a product, place, thing or politician is like the symbol he figuratively stands next to. Nike shoes are "good" because stars like Michael Jordan wear them, or toothpaste will make you popular because that's what happens in the commercial.

The Porn industry sells pornography to the masses by the con job of associating it with constitutional freedoms. This association would make our founding fathers turn over in their graves.

It's a con to sell products and politicians. Sadly, the shadier part of our economic culture is based on this tactic. This shallow magician's trick, as with all lies, leads to meaninglessness and despair.

The association con in terms of porn is not only bad, it is also an empty evil that can only mimic reality. It's men having imaginary relationships with artificially enhanced glossed-over images of what were once pictures of real women, betraying their most intimate selves and future relationships. The emptiness keeps multiplying.

Porn is not symbolic of real life, but a lifelike imitation of reality.

As Navrozov said, "There is no deeper conflict in history than that between these opposing views of art. 'Is art to serve reality and the individual under God or is it to serve [materialistic] realism and the masses."

The marketing and selling of porn brings us to Bill Clinton, who, despite promises to the contrary, disrupted the "obscenity prosecution" by Ronald Reagan's task force, which had the porn industry in serious trouble in the late '80s and early '90s.

Culture Wars editor E. Michael Jones said in the February 2001 issue, "This [Reagan] task force caused a major rollback of the porn industry during the late '80s and early '90s…. Florida, according to Sears, was on its way to becoming a porn-free state—except for one county, whose District Attorney inexplicably refused to prosecute cases. That county was Dade County and the name of the DA was Janet Reno and she became the Attorney General when William Jefferson Clinton took office in 1992. That event signaled the end of the federal task force to prosecute pornography."

Clinton lived the message. He was the presidential X-rated soap opera star for the $10 billion annual pornography industry.

Our society was willing to accept Clinton as an anti-hero. And as Ditko said, "an anti-hero corrupts the moral good."

His presidential movie star appeal and the porn industry's money helped his party by association to sell porn, homosexuality, abortion and masturbation all the way down to the elementary schools.

Mr. Clinton, 'There Is an Is'

A few years ago, I spoke with a director of a Texas crisis pregnancy center who has saved thousands of unborn babies. We spoke of a pro-life group whose top priority—to put it mildly—was not saving as many babies as possible. He said to stay away from them because they are "spiritual masturbators."

I love new word combinations, so I researched this term to see where it would take me. I found masturbation to be a good metaphor for the spiritual direction our society is taking.

"The ultimate direction of masturbation always has to be insanity," Norman Mailer said. "If one has, for example, the image of a beautiful sexy babe in masturbation, one still doesn't know whether one can make love to her in the flesh. All you know is that you can violate her in the brain.... But, if one has fought the good or evil fight and ended with the beautiful sexy dame...one has something real to build on."

Masturbation—as the pornography industry knows—is a profitable lie. For example, if someone says he had sex with a porn star and he didn't, it is a lie. If one *imagines* having sex with a porn star, it is still an untruth. The imagination is used to reach unreality.

In contrast with this abuse, the imagination can be used to reach into deep reality. As philosopher Edith Stein showed, truth can be found using the phenomenon of the imagination. As Thomas Aquinas also demonstrated, the mind can grasp the realities of love, truth and God using the phenomena of the imagination and reason. One need only read Shakespeare or G. K. Chesterton to see the imagination grasping deep truths.

Chesterton, in a book on Thomas Aquinas's philosophy, shows how the reason and imagination can work together to reveal the philosophical reality of being:

"A brilliant Victorian scientist delighted in declaring that the child does not see any grass at all; but only a sort of green mist reflected in a tiny mirror of the human eye.

"This piece of rationalism has always struck me as almost insanely irrational. If he is not sure of the existence of the grass, which he sees through the glass of a window, how on earth can he be sure of the existence of the retina, which he sees through the glass of a microscope.... [T]he child is aware of Ens [being]. Long before he knows that grass is grass, or self is self, he knows that something is something. Perhaps it would be best to say very emphatically [with a blow on the table], There is an Is...a thing cannot be and not be. Henceforth, in common or popular language, there is false and true."

The masturbator who imagines he is with the porn star is not in is—or, in common language, he is in falsehood. His body and imagination are moving—as moderns would say, progressing—but the direction of his mind is toward unreality. The porn addict and people like Clinton must always ask for the definition of 'is' because they are living in a lie.

Once one denies absolute truth and the law of identity, he will live in a lie. Ditko said, "Aristotle formulated the law of identity. A is A. A thing is what it is. It has a specific nature and identity. It cannot contradict itself and be a lie."

This said, our society has two directions it can go.

It can either go the Clintonian direction, toward the unreality of the pornography industry, which does not want an Is because then it would have to be morally responsible.

Or it can go in the direction of the reality that Ditko points to, where there is an Is, as well as the reality of God, love, beauty, free will, responsibility and the honorable hero.

Our society has this choice.

Actually, our society doesn't have this choice. Only each individual can make this choice. Our society needs you to be one of the millions of heroes who will bring us back to responsibility, truth, love and God.

Fred Martinez

Appendix 1

How to Save Unborn Babies in a Positive Way

A Complete Guide for Running a Successful Pro-life Home Visitation Campaign

Archangel Instructions

Introduction

We are Archangels in imitation of Gabriel, the Archangel.

Gabriel said to the Blessed Mother of Jesus and all mothers: "Do not be afraid, Mary, for you have found grace with God. Behold you shall conceive in your womb and shall bring forth a Son and you shall call His name Jesus." (Luke 1:30,31)

The babies you help save by home visitation are the baby Jesus because Jesus said, "Whatever you do to the least of my brethren you do to me."

Each mother should be thought of as a new Blessed Mother of Jesus.

What Is an Archangel?

An Archangel is a person who spreads the good news that God was an unborn baby and therefore all babies in the womb are of infinite value along with their mothers. The Archangel spreads the good news by home visiting.

What Is Home Visiting?

Home visiting is the prime work of the Archangel and it involves the following:

Step 1

Ring the bell or knock on the door. While you're waiting for an answer, say a "Hail Mary" for the home. If by the end of the "Hail Mary" no one has answered, leave the pro-life literature (especially information about crisis pregnancy centers) as well as chastity literature and go to the next home. Remember when you say the "Hail Mary" that it is the prayer of Gabriel to the Blessed Mother of Jesus. When they answer the door, say, "Hi, do you have 30 seconds?"

Step 2

When someone is interested (as are the vast majority), gently hold up the eleven-old-week model and say the following:
"This is an eleven- to twelve-week-old baby in the mother's womb. The vast majority of babies killed in abortions in the United States are this old or older. This baby is already a boy or a girl. His heart is already beating. His brain waves already work and he has fingerprints like you and me. This baby is the baby Jesus because Jesus said, 'Whatever you do to the least

of my brethren you do to me.' In fact this is what Jesus looked like when He was in His mother's womb. Do you think this little baby has the right to live?"

If they say "NO," say "Thank you" only and go to the next home.

The vast majority, however, says "Yes." In two model programs, one in California and the other in New Mexico, over 2,000 homes were visited, with 90 percent to 95 percent saying "yes" to the message and then receiving the pamphlets.

When they say "Yes," say "May I give these (pamphlets) to you in case you might know a young lady who might need help?" They all take the material.

Finally, say "Thank you" and keep following the Archangel Gabriel until you get to heaven.

Note: I'm not associated with any of the organizations listed below, but I've personally used all their products and can highly recommend them.

1. A model of 11- to 12-week-old unborn babies can be bought at:

PROJECT YOUNG ONE
2125 W. Lawn Ave.
Racine, WI 53405
(414) 634-8697

LIFE-SIZE MODEL OF UNBORN BABY.

Fred Martinez

Racine, Wisc.: Project "Young One." Affordable fetal models. Its life-size 11- to 12-week-old fetus (with wallet-sized card describing level of development) costs only $.30 each (quantity discounts above 2,000), plus $2 handling. Now available, a life-size plastic model of an unborn baby in the fourth month of development. Beautiful and realistic detail, firm feel. Order for pregnancy help centers, parishes, and schools ($7.50 each, plus $3.00 postage).

2. A video program covering all aspects of Fred Martinez's Archangel Home Visitation program can be purchased at:

The Apostolate for Family Consecration
3375 Rt. 36
Bloomingdale, OH 43910
1-800-FOR-MARY

3. You can learn more about the archangels in a set of three tapes called *The Three Archangels* by Fr. Ailbe O'Reilly. Send a check for $15.50 (P &H included) to:

Opus Sanctorum Angelorum
13800 Gratiot Avenue
Detroit, MI 48205
(313) 527-1739

Appendix 2

The following article appeared on NewsMax.com on August 12, 2002.

What Is VOTF's Real Agenda?
Fred Martinez

Recently, Voice of the Faithful (VOTF) became the news media's favorite "Catholic" lay organization to cure the Catholic Church of its sex abuse scandal.

The New York Times and *The Boston Globe* wrote glowing articles about this new "mainstream" Catholic organization. Even in Ireland and on the European landmass, newspapers were covering this "grassroots" group that started in a humble church basement.

VOTF claims it wants to democratize and subordinate the bishops to "lay participation." It also claims to be mainstream and conservative.

I received this e-mail from one of my readers asking me about VOTF's claims:

"Could you please direct me to a reliable assessment of the group Voice of the Faithful? A local 'chapter' is meeting this afternoon in Nashville, and it has been characterized by a local priest as 'just conservative Catholics who want some changes.'"

Voice of the Faithful and Gay & Lesbian Alliance Against Defamation

The only information I had about this "conservative Catholics" group was that a member of VOTF's steering committee was working closely with the homosexual spin group Gay & Lesbian Alliance Against Defamation (GLAAD).

On June 15 at the Dallas bishops meeting, homosexual activist Cathy Renna, writing for GLAAD's website, said that during a victory get-together, she met with "a number of familiar media faces" and Anne Barrett Doyle of the Coalition of Concerned Catholics, who is a member of the steering committee for the lay reform movement Voice of the Faithful.

According to Renna, "Anne was one of the first people I spoke with back in March when we were cultivating resources and contacts to offer media outlets.... Seeing Anne at the cathedral brought to mind how far we've come in the past months."

During those months, the media outlets, under the sway of gay activists like Renna and her friend Doyle, had censored George Will, Pope John Paul II's spokesman Dr. Joaquin Navarro-Valls, and the almost-all-conservative spokespersons in Dallas who attempted to report the "link between homosexuality and sexual abuse by priests," which *U.S. News & World Report* detailed before the media cover-up.

Earlier in the year, before the recent cover-up was solidified, *U.S. News & World Report* columnist John Leo wrote that studies have shown that 5 percent of priests or fewer fit the pedophile description. He said, "Most sexual victims of priests are teenage boys [abused in homosexual acts], according to one estimate. A study of Chicago's 2,200 priests identified 40 sexual abusers, only one of whom was a pedophile."

Now, just because one of the VOTF steering committee members was working closely with the Gay & Lesbian Alliance spin group to censor George Will, Pope John Paul II's spokesman and the Catholic conservative spokespersons at the Dallas bishops meeting doesn't necessarily mean that the VOTF isn't a "mainstream" and "conservative Catholic" group.

One must examine the "mainstream" and "conservative Catholic" priests that are supporting VOTF before making any judgments about that group. Unfortunately, not one single mainstream and conservative orthodox Catholic priest supports the group.

Voice of the Faithful and the Liberal Richard P. McBrien

However, Fr. Richard P. McBrien, a professor of theology at the University of Notre Dame, put his support for the organization into an article in *The Tidings* on July 19 called "Listening to the 'Voice of the Faithful.'" As all mainstream and conservative Catholics know, McBrien is one of the most liberal Catholic theologians in the U.S.

Fred Martinez

McBrien has shown that he is 100 percent opposed to the official teachings of the Catholic Church when it counters the gay and lesbian movement's agenda.

The official Catechism of the Catholic Church states in section 2357 that "homosexual acts are intrinsically disordered...under no circumstances can they be approved."

Also, the Sacred Congregation for Religious in Rome in 1961 stated: "Those affected by the perverse inclination to homosexuality or pederasty should be excluded from religious vows and ordination." Roman Catholic Faithful President Stephen Brady said, "The Church directive has never been rescinded and is still officially in force."

But McBrien, in an April 5, 2002, *Tidings* piece, disagreed with those who hold the official teachings of the Church, calling them "homophobes who look upon gays as disreputable souls held in the grip of the worst sort of moral perversion."

He then went on to attack Pope John Paul II's spokesman, Dr. Joaquin Navarro-Valls, for wanting to get "rid of gay priests."

The Vatican spokesman said homosexual ordination might be invalid in the same way a marriage can be annulled on the grounds that it was invalid from the start. For example, a woman who marries a homosexual can get her marriage annulled on those grounds.

McBrien, in his anger at Pope John Paul II's spokesman, revealed how widespread the homosexual problem is in the U.S.

He wrote: "A few priests have privately observed that, if this [homosexual ordination annulment] were actually to happen, the Roman Catholic Church might lose two-thirds of its priests under the age of 45 and some bishops as well. At the same time, many of its seminaries could be emptied of all but a handful of students."

A Large Percentage of the Liberal U.S. Priests Are Homosexual

Some orthodox Catholics have observed that the Vatican and some Latin American bishops are naïve as to how big a percentage of the liberal U.S. bishops and U.S. priests are homosexual.

The statement by one of the most respected liberal U.S. Catholic theologians that "two-thirds of its priests under the age of 45 and some bishops as well" are homosexual will hopefully open the eyes of those who are naïve about the "gay movement's" influence over liberal priests and certain VOTF lay Catholic theologians.

Lay Catholic theologian Thomas Groome, Senior Professor of Theology and Religious Education at Boston College, who has been a featured speaker at VOTF meetings in the Boston Diocese, is—like McBrien—in favor of homosexual ordination.

On March 21, 2002, according to *The Miami Herald*, Groome said homosexuality is rampant in the nation's seminaries. The *Herald* quoted the lay theologian as saying, "A well-balanced gay person can make a fine priest." "Having been 'inside,' I knew lots

125

of gays and philanderers. I've known hundreds of priests and never known a pedophile. They hide themselves well," said Groome.

According to the Boston Diocese *Sacred Heart Bulletin*, in June Groome gave his lay participation talk on "Doing Theology Ourselves" at St. Eulalia's Parish (Manion Hall) on Ridge Street, Winchester, which is a major chapter of VOTF in the diocese.

The Rev. Victor LaVoie, a Strong Supporter of Voice of the Faithful

The Boston Globe said St. Eulalia parishioners praised pastor Rev. Victor LaVoie as "a strong supporter of the Voice of the Faithful."

One must consider the Rev. LaVoie to be unfaithful to the teachings of the Catholic Church on homosexuality if he has ex-priest (and McBrien clone) Groome—now turned lay spokesman—speaking at his parish.

On July 26, 2002, LaVoie became "the 17th priest the archdiocese [of Boston] has removed over allegations of sexual abuse since January," according to the *Globe*.

The parishioners who supported VOTF also support their pastor. The *Globe* said, "Hundreds of parishioners attended a prayer meeting at St. Eulalia's last night to discuss LaVoie's suspension and to pray for him."

This is still the U.S. and LaVoie is innocent until proven guilty. So to be fair, the archdiocese's review board is still investigating all the priests suspended on credible allegations.

It has not yet announced any decisions on any of the cases, including the pastor of St. Eulalia. It is good that LaVoie has been suspended and it will be good that he and others spend time in jail if the allegations are true.

VOTF and Liberals Use Church Scandal as a Power Grab

Voice of the Faithful and other liberals, however, were not so fair with other priests alleged to have committed sex abuse who they have been using as a political football to forward their lay participation and homosexual agenda.

Nor have VOTF or the liberals been so fair with the Vatican when it brought forward the real reason for the vast majority of the sex abuse scandal.

It is safe to say that one cannot find one liberal Catholic who will support the whole statement of the 1961 Sacred Congregation for Religious, which stated: "Those affected by the perverse inclination to homosexuality or pederasty should be excluded from religious vows and ordination."

In fact, the pro-gay *National Catholic Reporter* (*NCR*), which is "the" newspaper of U.S. liberal Catholics—and a strong supporter of McBrien—has been pushing Voice of the Faithful as a mainstream organization for months.

On May 24, in an article called "Church in Crisis: Scandal Diminishes Churches' Clout," *NCR* said, "Not only are pastors running weekly notices about Voice of the Faithful's meetings—explaining the group's mission and goals—but some are assisting laywomen and men in establishing parish voice chapters in their respective churches."

In the very same article *NCR* said, "While these legislative developments indicate a waning of the [Boston] archdiocese's influence on relatively mainstream social policy matters, perhaps an even stronger measure of the cardinal's diminishing political clout came last month at a joint state House and Senate committee hearing. Two priests publicly opposed the church's position. The topic was same-sex marriage...."

"While many of the gay community's longstanding political, legal and religious allies gathered in the statehouse to oppose the gay civil-rights setback, they were joined—for the first time in state history—by two Roman Catholic priests."

These statements on VOTF and homosexuality by the most respected liberal U.S. Catholic newspaper and the Rev. McBrien, the respected liberal theologian, show that VOTF is not mainstream, as James Likoudis says.

"Richard P. McBrien oozes with admiration for this group [Voice of the Faithful] seeking to restructure the Church, democratize it, gain financial control of it, and subordinate our Bishops to this new lay class of secular feudal lords and professionals," Catholics United for the Faith's Likoudis said.

"It's a power grab under the guise of more 'lay participation' and is made up of those dissenting liberals and radicals who do not like Catholic moral teaching but do like Dignity and GLAAD [radical homosexual organizations]."

Appendix 3

The following article appeared in the Conservative Monitor of March 2001.

Public Schools Unsafe at Any Price
Fred Martinez

The nightmares of Columbine and Santana high schools mark a turning point, as did the Kennedy assassination. The assassination prolonged a myth, while the school massacres may be ending a myth.

The myth of Camelot—the lie of the perfect presidential family—seemed to usher in the sexual revolution, whereas the ending of the dysfunctional presidential family coincided with the end of the myth of "the good American education."

Market researcher C. Britt Beemer thinks the "Columbine factor" has changed our country's mindset. His surveys show that 70 percent of parents now think danger in schools will continue to increase. "Informed parents" are dissatisfied with public schools' drugs, peer pressure and poor teaching. He sees a trend toward single-income families and homeschooling.

After 50 years of feminist propaganda, parents appear to be realizing that children are smarter and healthier when they spend more time with their parents. After 150 years of education propaganda, parents are beginning to see public schools as unsafe to the moral, intellectual and physical well-being of kids.

John Taylor Gatto—former New York City and State Teacher of the Year—documents how the education system purposely created a mass of illiterates. In *The Underground History of American Education* he states that in 1840—before public education—93 percent to 100 percent of both poor and rich had "complex literacy." But since "compulsory" schools began, each succeeding generation has become more illiterate. After WWII—with increased funding of public schools—black illiteracy doubled and white illiteracy quadrupled.

Why the "dumbing-down"? The one "well-documented" change was the American schools' massive conversion to "non-phonetic ways of teaching reading." The dumbing-down was followed by violence.

Justice Department records show that violent criminals are overwhelmingly (80 percent) illiterate. Since WWII, as illiteracy increased, so did crime, out-of-wedlock births quadrupled, and, in the '60s, "bizarre violence...became common."

The '60s saw the schools' replacement of morality and discipline with reinforcement schedules. There was no right or wrong, only the sterile therapeutic concepts of "positive and negative reinforcement" to maintain the "social order."

As "planned smiles," "stern looks," "self-esteem" and "aggression management" replaced the Ten Commandments, was it any wonder that school security guards and metal detectors became a growth industry?

Was it any wonder that teachers with heart, like Jaime Escalante of *Stand and Deliver* fame, were weeded out? Is it any wonder that the two or three really good teachers we remember were the exceptions, not the rule? It is a wonder that it took us this long to figure it out.

*****

Both Jaime Escalante and John Taylor Gatto were weeded out of the public school system. (Look these two educators up on the Internet—they were both forced out.)

I included this article because it shows the hypocrisy of liberals. While they claim to be the only ones helping minorities and the poor, they force out true educators such as Latino Escalante and Teacher of the Year Gatto, who were truly helping the Latinos and other minorities as well as poor whites in Los Angeles and New York.

While we must pay tribute to the numerous public school teachers who quietly stay in the system doing good despite the system, these two teachers are examples of Spider-Man–like heroes, who, rather than allowing themselves to be cognitively redefined into a "culture of teamwork," were willing to lose their jobs.

Remember what the very respected scholar Edgar H. Schein of MIT's Sloan School of Management said about the process in his essay "Organizational

Learning as Cognitive Re-definition: Coercive Persuasion Revisited":

"It may seem absurd to the reader to draw an analogy between the coercive persuasion in political prisons and a new leader announcing that he or she is going 'to change the culture....'"

"The coercive element is not as strong. More people will simply leave before they change their cognitive structures, but if they have a financial stake or a career investment in the organization, they face the same pressure to 'convert' that the prisoner did."

Like Spider-Man in the movie, and Escalante as well as Gatto in real life, you and I must be willing to lose something to save the children and those we most love—as another hero did 2,000 years ago.

Book Purchasing Information

To order more copies of *The Hidden Axis of Evil*, send check or money order to:

1stbooks Library
1663 Liberty Drive, Suite #200
Bloomington, IN 47403
888-280-7715

Orders can be made by credit card at www.therealaxis.com.

Orders can be made by credit card also at bkorders@1stbooks.com, www.amazon.com, or www.BarnesandNoble.com. If you go to any of these three sites, just type Fred Martinez or *The Hidden Axis of Evil* in the Search window.

Bookstores or others wishing to buy wholesale may order by going to bkorders@1stbooks.com or calling 888-280-7715. You can also order from Ingram. The ISBN is 1410746186.

Also, if you want to buy *The Hidden Axis of Evil* as an e-book, go to bkorders@1stbooks.com or www.therealaxis.com. The cost is $4.00.

Fred Martinez

About the Author

Fred Martinez is the religion editor of the online Conservative Monitor and a reporter with the *San Francisco Faith*. He was a Special Commentary columnist for the website NewsMax.com during the height of the Catholic scandal in 2002, and has been published in American and British publications, as well as having some of his writings translated into Lithuanian.

In 1985, his philosophical writings opened the opportunity to study for a doctorate at the International Academy of Philosophy in Liechenstein, Europe. Instead, following what he considered to be the call of God, he founded the Juan Diego Society, which is still helping women in crisis pregnancies. He also produced and hosted the Catholic television show *Latino Love* in 1989.

Martinez has appeared as a Catholic and political science expert on the *Apostolate for Family Consecration* program on EWTN Catholic Television Network, the Pat Campbell show (WOMP-AM, Ohio), the Chuck Morse show (WROL-AM, Boston) and the (former Vatican) Ambassador Ray Flynn show (WROL-AM, Boston).

He received a Bachelor's degree in Political Science and a Master's in Public Affairs at San Jose State University.

Fred Martinez can be contacted at mrtnzfred@aol.com.